PASSION TO CAREERS:

Nine steps to *BUILD A SUCCESSFUL CAREER*
from your *PASSION*

GUGU KHAZI

First published in 2019.

ISBN: 978-1-86922-824-8
eISBN: 978-1-86922-825-5 (ePDF)

Published by KR Publishing
P O Box 3954
Randburg
2125
Republic of South Africa

Tel: (011) 706-6009
Fax: (011) 706-1127
E-mail: orders@knowres.co.za
Website: www.kr.co.za

Typesetting, layout and design: Cia Joubert, cia@knowres.co.za
Cover design: Marlene de'Lorme, marlene@knowres.co.za
Editing and proofreading: Valda Strauss, valda@global.co.za
Project management: Cia Joubert, cia@knowres.co.za

Contents

About the Author

Gugu Khazi is an author, career coach, and international speaker on Personal Career Management as well as leadership. She holds a Master's in Business Management as well as an MSc in Industry, Trade & Development from Milpark Business School and the University of Manchester respectively.

She has over 20 years of experience as a senior HR leader in various international businesses such as Kimberly-Clark and The Coca-Cola Company both in Southern Africa and the United Kingdom. Her journey in finding a career that she likes and helping others manage their careers inspired her to write *Passion To Careers* to share her knowledge with others across the world on how to build successful and fulfilling careers.

Gugu is now running her own consulting firm focusing on helping businesses develop leaders that are more than "job providers" and are "career providers".

Introduction

Do you get the feeling that your working life is not fulfilling your true potential? That your skills, passion and unique wisdom are wasted in your current career? You're not alone – and it's not your fault. But you *can* change your perspective and change your life by discovering a new way to think about jobs, work, and achieving your dreams.

This book is rooted in my personal experience and written with the intention of giving you the tools you need to change the way you look at your career. I have learnt a lot from my own journey towards finding a career that supports my passion. This journey, and everything I learned from it, has been enriched by the combined effort of the thousands of people I met, worked with, and helped develop in their own careers over the past twenty years working as an HR leader.

After experiencing and observing the journeys of many other people, I have discovered that the way we look at the world of work often limits our potential for a truly fulfilling career. I urge that we shift our focus from how the individual can benefit the company; instead, let's concentrate on how to best support and inspire an individual's personal passion and skills. By doing so, we can create careers which pave the way for growth and progress – for individuals, businesses, and the culture of work in general.

To put it bluntly, I propose that we have been looking at jobs and careers in a wrong way. The emphasis is always on the company, the employer, or to use typical HR jargon, the "business requirements". This refers to the skills and experience the company requires from any individual it hires. Little care is given to the needs of the person, the candidate; the employee and their passions. When companies recruit they look for someone who will meet their list of requirements, rather than someone who is passionate about a particular aspect of the business. And I believe they're missing a trick – because passionate employees are productive employees.

We are conditioned to fit ourselves into the world of work rather than create a working life that suits us from an early age. You might hope that schools would help children realise their passions, but as personal strengths expert Marcus Buckingham[1] observes, "schools only want to make sure that everybody learns what everybody is supposed to learn". We then go on to inhabit similarly uninspiring work environments which are not connected to our passions because the main concern (of the employer) is that we have the key skills and knowledge to perform and get the job done. As Buckingham observes, everyone in your life has expectations and demands that are not necessarily connected to your strengths and passion.

The problem with this approach is that individuals must mould and package themselves to fit the company requirements. Your personal likes and dislikes, your passions, and your self-identified calling in life often go unacknowledged. The inevitable result of this is that individuals are hired based on what the company needs, and not on the individual's talent or strengths. So you – the employee – find yourself moving from one job to another, or from one company to another, looking for an indefinable "something" or a seemingly unattainable sense of satisfaction. On the other hand, companies have lost an opportunity to pull together an engaged workforce, fuelled by their passion.

A Gallup 2016 report on "how millennials want to work and live" revealed that younger generations are currently less satisfied and engaged at work compared to their older counterparts. It showed that 21% of the Millennials reported having looked for a job in the past year – three times more than Baby Boomers and Gen X. Furthermore, only 29% of this generation is happy at work. The rest are checked-out as not putting their energy and passion into their work.[2]

This report resonates with my views and experience on the issue. There was a point in my life when I would spend an average of one year in each company I worked for. I had good jobs with successful employers, but I couldn't shake the feeling that something was missing. In each new role, I would spend eight months finding my feet before the frustrating feeling that I was wasting my time crept back in. It took some time, but the repetition of this pattern led me to realise that there had to be more that I needed to fix – simply changing companies wasn't working for me. It was making my CV look bad and I was running out of explanations as to why I was changing jobs so frequently. I had to look deeper into what my passion was, what I *really* wanted to do, in order to experience that tremendous excitement that comes with doing something you truly love and care about. I needed to find my passion. And it was at that point that I stopped the cycle of perpetual job-hopping.

Unfortunately, most people are not lucky enough to realise this early on in their career. In fact, companies today accept that retaining employees for longer periods of time is increasingly unrealistic. So they plan for this, making financial and staffing provisions in anticipation of a high staff turnover. This is further exacerbated by the emerging belief that the new generation of millennials will be serial job-hoppers, as they are already marked as being desirous of extreme variation and the stimulation of change.

Personally, I remain unconvinced by these assertions. I believe that the problem with job dissatisfaction has traversed generations, the only difference being in how different generations have dealt with it, or have failed to deal with it altogether. Older generations believed in the value of loyalty to a company, and were incentivised by employers and the state to remain in jobs for longer periods, regardless of whether they enjoyed their work.

The younger generations are working in a different environment. Loyalty is not incentivised or rewarded, and many companies offer very limited opportunities for progression and minimal job security. As a result, we are seeing an increase in the number of people moving jobs and companies frequently.

So, why this drastic change? Why are people not loyal anymore? Why are we becoming serial job-hoppers? As well as changes in the broader economic environment, I believe this is seeded in how we choose our careers from the very beginning. As individuals, we look for jobs before we have an in-depth understanding of our passions, what drives us, and what our personal ambitions (beyond surviving) are. Companies encourage this by hiring purely based on self-interest, without considering whether they are best placed to support the development of their employees' careers.

The job-seeking and job-filling conversation does not take heed of your personal dreams, ambition, and passion. Interestingly, a backlash to this is emerging – a fast-spreading belief that in order to have a career which is aligned with your passion you must become an entrepreneur. It is rare to meet someone in traditional employment who is passionate about their job.

I argue that you *can* find a job which you are truly passionate about. A job which is exciting and stimulating. A job that you will look forward to dedicating your time to, every single day. But to find that job, you need to look at your career in a new light.

This book will change the way you look at your job and career. It will guide you in developing a job-hunting process tailored to your individuality, and it is a catalyst for passion-driven recruitment. I hold firm that if you approach your career with the intention of finding your *passion* instead of finding a *job*, you will be able to build a sustainable and soul-nourishing career for yourself. I hope that the in-the-trenches employment stories I share in this book will expand your understanding of why it's so important to take control of managing your career.

Crucially, I will outline a nine-step programme which will allow you to identify your most profound strengths and personal passions – and then discover how to use these as the foundations on which to build your ideal career. You do not have to stop being employed to pursue your passion; you need to make your passion the starting point for your employment.

For individuals, the benefits of finding and developing a career based on passion are immense. But businesses have yet to realise the benefits of investing in the inspiration of their staff. According to Theresa Szczuka, a well-known author on issues related to passion and purpose, the important source of competitive advantage in the twenty- first century will come from individuals and organisations that unleash the power of passion.[3]

This book is for you if:

1. You find yourself job hopping, looking for a career you can connect to.

2. You do not feel fulfilled by the job you have.

3. You do not earn what you believe you deserve to earn.

4. You do not feel enthused by the work you are doing.

5. You have a confused person in your life who is not sure about what career to choose and despite wanting to help them, you are unsure about where to begin.

Immerse yourself in discovering *you* as you apply these nine steps to finding and progressing in the job you are passionate about. This is an actionable guide to realising your potential and achieving success in your career.

Finally, if you have any questions or if you would like to connect with me, please contact me at gugu.khazi@ passiontocareers.com

The nine-step model

You want a career that excites you, that makes you proud, and which taps into your passion. You want to feel inspired and alive every day. And this is not unattainable because if you're doing what you love, you'll do it well.

My nine-step model has been developed over years of work as an HR leader, helping others create work lives aligned with their dreams, and it will allow you to identify and pursue the right career for you.

Before we explore each step in detail, here is a brief summary which outlines the complete journey. You can use this to refer back to when you need to remind yourself of how far you've come, or which step you need to focus on next.

Step 1

Identify your passion. What do you like? What do you enjoy doing? What are you good at?

This is a critical step because it determines the direction you will take with your career.

Step 2

Learn before you can earn. Take action by gaining an understanding of how you can learn and develop skills associated with your passion.

Step 3

Find a mentor. This is a person who will guide you through your career journey. Here, I outline how you can find a mentor, and how to get the most from your mentoring.

Step 4

Establish career choices. In this chapter, I provide you with a guide on what you need to consider when you explore opportunities in the job market, and how to ensure that the choices you make early on have a positive impact on the direction and progression of your career.

Step 5

Prepare for the interview. This step covers inside information on how the interview process works; how you can prepare yourself for interviews; and what questions you need to ask to make sure the job in question is aligned with your passion.

Step 6

Grow your passion. This step details methods to ensure that you continue to develop and nurture your passion after you've secured a job that ignites your fire.

Step 7

Reinvent your career. If a job that was once aligned with your passion no longer fulfils you, don't worry. In this step, you'll find out how to transform or transition your career if the passion wanes.

Step 8

Build a legacy to be proud of. Here, we look at how to build your career and prepare to monetise it later.

Step 9

Monetise your passion. This last step teaches you how to consolidate all that you have learnt and experienced throughout your career, packaging it in a way that can be offered to others to support their success while generating revenue for you.

How to use the nine-step model

The nine-step model is designed around an expectation that you are prepared to take action to build your career. It has clear guidelines on the steps you need take, as well as actionable tools to create your own personal action plan. The book is very interactive, with self-reflective questions that will help you get to the answers you are looking for. The weekly planner will help keep you accountable to your career goals.

The chapters do not necessarily have to be read in chronological order; however, if you are just starting your career it would be best to begin from the first chapter. Starting from the first chapter might also refine your concept of what a passion is and how it can align with your career. If you already have an established career, you will benefit from the steps 6, 7, 8 and 9.

I wish you enormous success in building your ideal career using the *Passion to Career* nine-step model!

Gugu Khazi

Step One

DISCOVER YOUR PASSION

"What would you do if you did not need to work for money?"

Throughout my school years I wanted to become a social worker. I had observed my aunt thriving and changing people's lives in this role, and although I didn't really understand what exactly the job entailed, I knew it was about helping people. Since helping people was my passion, I understood that Social Work was my ultimate calling. When the time came for me to choose my university subjects, it was a natural choice. It was what I had wanted to do since very early on in my life. But during the fourth year of studies I realised that while helping others was my passion, Social Work was not the only way to do so. The more I learned and the closer I came to embarking on that career, the clearer it became that it was not my passion.

What is passion?

Passion is defined in myriad ways. Marcus Buckingham[4], for example, refers to it as "your genius" – a combination of strengths that are deeply a part of who you are. Similarly, American author Robert Greene[5] explains that each one of us possesses an inner force that guides us toward Life's Task – "What you are meant to accomplish in the time that you have to live". Typically this force is much clearer to us in childhood. It is what guided us toward activities and subjects that fit what we are naturally inclined to – activities that sparked our curiosity and have us naturally gravitating towards them. However, as we grow older and life removes all the innocence, this instinct winds down as we are influenced by what culture and sometimes our parents expect us to be.

Although passion may be described in different ways, it's clear that there is a common agreement on the existence of innate strength and intuition which guide you towards activities that make you feel vibrantly alive. Because these innate strengths and intuitions fade as we grow older, the key to career success is reigniting your connection with your passion, and building your working life around it.

How do you find your passion?

To understand your passion, you will need to understand your talents. Marcus Buckingham sees this as the recurring pattern of thoughts, feelings and behaviours that tend to direct you towards particular activities that you like.[4] These are the behaviours that you instinctively possess, such as being empathetic, being competitive, being charming, and so on. For each of us, these behaviours feel so natural that we tend to take them for granted and think they are common sense. Because of this enduring nature, your talents determine how well and how often you can do something. Your passion comes out when you engage in activities which utilise your talents. It is, therefore, an obvious conclusion that for you to find your passion, you need to be clear about what your talents are.

Your talents cause you to react in a particular way when you do something related to them. They evoke a positive feeling and *this* is the place from which your passion radiates. You can feel it immediately; and importantly, others can sense it too!

Discovering your passion is a journey rather than a single epiphany. A marathon, as opposed to a sprint. There are a number of ways to uncover where your passions lie. One of the methods that I can encourage based on my own experience and on observing others, is to follow your curiosity.

What are you curious about?

Leena Varshaskaya, founder and CEO of Wanelo Digital Mall, believes that by following your curiosity you will discover the unique motivations that separate you from others. But *how* do you follow your curiosity? Start by asking yourself this:

What would you do if you had all the money in the world and did not need to work for a living?

While you consider this question, accept that your answers might sound frivolous and impractical at first. Normally, under any other circumstances, this is the point at which we would stop entertaining that idea and move on. But this is a critical step towards discovering your passion – do not stop!

Steve Jobs is often presented as an example of someone who followed his curiosity and ended up turning it into something huge. He had a curiosity for typefaces, which then led to him attending (at the time) useless classes on typography and design. Far from being a waste of time, however, the knowledge he acquired became an essential part of *Apple*, as well as its core differentiator in the market place. If we were to point out one thing that makes Apple different, we would probably mention elegance and simplicity in every aspect of design. The fruit of Steve Jobs' curiosity.

The moral of the story here is that the key to discovering your passion is noticing what sparks your curiosity, and seeing where that curiosity might take you – even if it seems pointless in the moment. It is this curiosity which will lead you to discover not only your passion, but by extension, your true calling.

Let's do a practical exercise. Write down five things that you are curious about at the moment:

What are you curious about?
1.
2.
3.
4.
5.

What do people "pick your brains" on?

In some instances, others see our passion more clearly than we do. You can harness the power of their observations by considering the questions that you are frequently asked by your friends, family and colleagues. This is what I call the "pick your brains test".

What do people ask to *pick your brains* on most of the time? At work, it's likely to be something related to your particular professional role; but in informal settings, it is probably something related to your areas of interest and passion.

For example, I'm constantly asked questions like: "Should I take this job?" and "Should I study this?" and "Is it time to look for another job?" In short, people believe in my expertise when it comes to finding and building a career so they're eager to pick my brains on this subject.

Do people ever pick your brains? List areas that you are often asked for advice on below:

1.

2.

3.

4.

5.

Find your passion, find your Ikigai

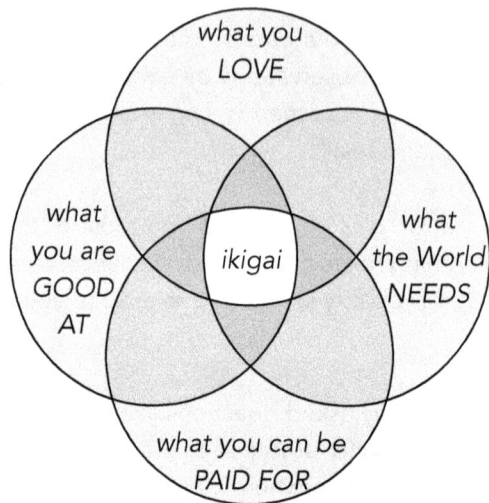

Figure 1.1 "Venn Diagram" by Hector Garcia and Frances Miralles, Translated by Heather Cleary, based on a diagram by Mark Winn; from IKIGAI THE JAPANESE SECRET TO A LONG AND HAPPY LIFE by Hector Garcia and Frances Miralles. Translation copy ©2017 by Penguin Random House LLC. Used by permission of Penguin Books, an imprint of Penguin Publishing Group, a division of Penguin Random House LLC. All rights reserved.

According to Japanese cultural beliefs, we each have Ikigai. Translated literally, *iki* means life and *gai* describes value or worth. Indirectly it refers to a reason for being, which can be adjusted or transformed over the years.[6] In practice, it means finding a reason to believe your life is worth living. Some people find this easy, while others are endlessly searching for this profound insight – even though, really, they have it within them already. Having a strong sense of Ikigai – the place where passion, mission, vocation, and profession intersect – means that each day is infused with meaning. You will experience this when the activities you love doing connect with what you are good at and *your passion* comes alive. When the activities you enjoy are aligned with the skills that are in demand in the world, *your mission* becomes clearer. When you can offer your skills to meet a specific demand, *your vocation is revealed*. Lastly, when the tasks you enjoy connect with what you are really good at, *your ideal profession* becomes clear. These are the building block of *your Ikigai*.

6

A study conducted by professor Toshimasa Sone and his colleagues, at Tohoku University, surveyed over 43,000 Japanese adults between the ages of 40 and 49. Among the questions asked one was about Ikigai: "Do you have Ikigai in your life?"[6]

The responses were varied; ranging from yes, no, to uncertain. The researchers followed up with participants over a seven-year period and found that 3,048 of the participants had died during that time. Among those whose lives had ended, a significant number was made up of those who had not reported experiencing a sense of Ikigai – compared with a much lower number of deaths among those participants who *had* felt a sense of Ikigai.

This study confirms a phenomenon long observed in Japan, that people who have a clear life purpose channelled through their career and vocation (Ikigai) are more likely to outlive those who don't have a clear life purpose.

What makes you flow?

Flow, also known as 'being in the zone', refers to the pleasure, delight and creativity you experience when you are fully immersed in life. It is a state in which you are so involved in an activity that nothing else seems to matter. It's almost as if time stops passing in the usual way. You feel challenged, you draw on your skills, enjoy the moment and stretch your capabilities.

Normally, the experience itself is so enjoyable that people will find ways to access their f low even at great cost, for the sheer sake of it. The key to achieving the state of flow is to have a meaningful challenge aligned to your passion. This is evident in the study by a Hungarian-American psychologist – Mihalay Csikszentmilalyi – who interviewed many experts in various fields, from composers and artists to tradesmen and chefs.[7] He found that many of them, in spite of differences in profession or culture, identified a similar concept of flow in relation to their careers. Many mentioned a sense of complete absorption in the task at hand, causing them to neglect physical needs including hunger, thirst, and sleep. They also remarked that time became irrelevant, feeling like only a few minutes had passed when they had in reality been engaged in an activity for hours. In addition, the interviewees took great pleasure in the activity they were engaged in, often describing something akin to spontaneous waves of joy and satisfaction.

The questions to ask yourself here, are:

- What are the activities that take you to the state of flow?

- Why do these activities drive you to flow?

- Do you flow more when you do these activities alone or with others?

- Do you flow more when you do movement activities or thinking activities?

By answering these questions, you will move closer to finding the passion that drives your life.

Identify your interests

Interest refers to those activities that you want to know or learn more about. Understanding your passion begins with knowing your interests. Interests are not only discovered, they can also be developed. In fact, we spend our lifetime developing and cultivating our interests. So, how can you identify your interests?

The most common framework for identifying interests is the Hollands RIASEC model.[8] The model asserts that most people's interests can be categorised into a combination of six personality types: Realistic, Investigative, Artistic, Social, Enterprising, and Conventional (commonly abbreviated with the acronym RIASEC). Each type is characterised by a collection of preferred activities, beliefs, abilities, values, and characteristics.

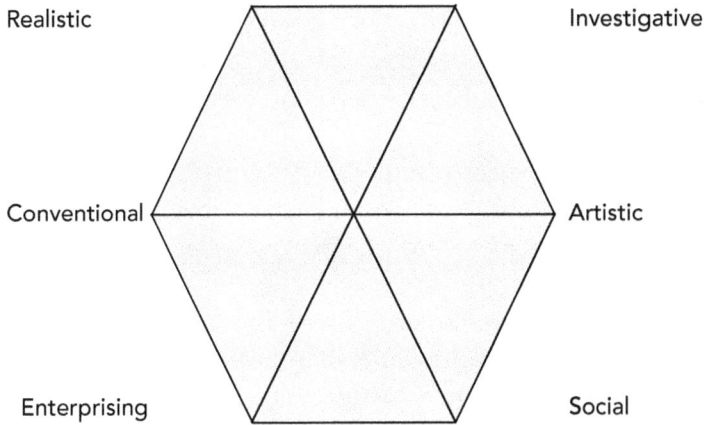

Realistic   Investigative

Conventional   Artistic

Enterprising   Social

John Holland, an American psychologist who developed the RIASEC framework, believes that as individuals we seek out work environments which will allow us to exercise these abilities and pursue our interests, while feeling free to express our personal attitudes and values.[8] It is safe to conclude that only when we do work in the areas of our interests will our passion shine through. Most people's interests are a combination of the following six personality types:

- Realistic – People with realist interests like working mainly with their hands making, fixing, assembling or building things, using and operating equipment, tools or machines.

- Investigative – People with investigative interests like to discover and research ideas, observe, investigate and experiment, ask questions and solve questions.

- Artistic – People with artistic interest like using words, art, music or drama to express themselves, communicate or perform or they like to create or design things.

- Social – People with social interests like working with people to teach, train, inform, help, treat, heal, cure, serve and greet. They are concerned for others' well-being and welfare.

- Enterprising – People with enterprising interests like meeting people, leading, talking to and influencing others, encouraging others, working in business.

- Conventional – People who like working indoors and at tasks that involve organising and being accurate, following procedures, working with data or numbers, planning work and events.

The intention of the Hollands (Self-Directed Search questionnaire) RIASEC assessment tools is to help people understand their interests and match those to a work environment that is aligned with their interests.

I have provided you with the RIASEC self-assessment tool in the toolkit (pages 124 – 126) – use it to determine your interests and work environments in which you are most likely to enjoy practising your craft.

You now have a number of effective techniques you can use to explore your passion. If you use these to understand who you are and what your interests are, you will confidently match these to careers, work environment and employers aligned to your passion.

How do you match your passion to your career?

Getting to know your passion is a great start to building a successful career. But it's just the beginning. The next challenge is to turn your passion into your work. This requires an understanding of the careers available to choose from, and an understanding of how these options could meet your needs.

As well as a vast array of careers available across all industries, there are also new careers – and new industries – developing all the time. It's impossible to be aware of every single option available to you.

Most of us begin a job hunt by looking at jobs currently being advertised, and base our career decisions on what we find. Based on the jobs on offer, we apply and eventually we're hired into a particular advertised position. I call this approach an *Outside-in approach*. This means that you are starting your career journey based on influences external to yourself – and I do not recommend this approach. It requires you to look at what others are offering and fitting yourself into the perimeters they have defined; which means you're likely to be squashing yourself into an ill-fitting box.

I know what you're thinking. Of course you have to make sure that you are marketable for jobs as advertised by companies and you have no way of influencing or pre-empting their requirements. We'll get to that later. What is important at this stage is to begin your career journey by focusing on yourself.

And you can do that by starting with an *Inside-out approach*. This involves looking at traits, passions and experiences that you possess and reflecting on how you can match those to available careers. I like this approach because it centers on you, who you are, what you like, and what you can offer to the world.

So, how do you start from your inside-out perspective?

Inside -Out perspective	Outside-In perspective
Focus is on you and what you can offer	Focus is on what is available in the market
Purpose is to match who you are and what you are good at to what the world needs	Purpose is to shape yourself to fit into what the world requires
Requires you to know your personality traits, your passions and your goals	Requires you to demonstrate fit through qualifications, experiences and profession
The outcome is finding jobs and building a career aligned to your strengths and your passion which lead to an enjoyable, long-lasting career	The outcome is good career based on expectations from others that you might not enjoy at the end of the day
Leads to more engagement, productivity and proven success	Leads to job dissatisfaction, disengagement and limited success

Figure 2.1 Difference between the Inside-out and Outside-in approach to choosing a career

Using the Inside-out approach to choose your career

The components of an inside-out approach tap into your inner self. These can be your passion, personality traits, strengths and interests.

I once worked with a client named Amanda, who could not believe her luck when she was offered a job as a property development consultant. The job was one of the first that she found available on the market when she decided she needed to change roles, and it paid well.

After accepting the job, she came to realise that it did not have the level of client engagement and interactions that she had anticipated and looked forward to. She did not enjoy the back-end developer work that she had to do. She told me "I rather liked working on finished properties ready to be sold to customers." She realised the job was not aligned to her strengths. Despite being dissatisfied with the job's capacity to feed her passion, she stayed longer than she should have because the pay was good.

However, each time she encountered a problem or challenge she was reminded that she did not like what she was doing. Six months into her new role she decided to quit and go back to her previous job. All it took for her to realise that money was not worth compromising herself for was a boss who did not recognise her for the effort she was making to deliver results. Because Amanda's career choice was based on external motivators, it was not sustainable when the job became challenging. These motivators could not carry her through difficulties. Why? Because the external motivations were not linked to any of her inner inspirations, her strengths, passion and personality traits.

Self-reflection Questions

1. I believe my talents are ...

2. People always ask me for help in the following areas...

3. If I did not have to work for a living, I would follow this passion of mine ...

4. Based on my RIASEC assessment (pages 124 to 126) my top 3 career interests are ...

Common Blockers to Connecting with your Passion

The fact that over 75% of working adults are dissatisfied with their jobs and are passive job seekers continuously seeking greener pastures is an indication that there is a mismatch.

What could be causing this mismatch, what could be blocking us from pursuing our passion and building our careers around the work we love? Fear is one of the main blockers in following your passion.

Think about how difficult it can be to deviate from expectation and choose to do something that you feel is aligned with your passion and talent. There have been many times when I have found myself in positions where I want to pursue something big and scary and the temptation to settle for less and live a comfortable life is huge. At times I have overcome the fear and pursued my goal and other times I have succumbed to the fear. I have had numerous failed attempts to change my career and transition to doing work that I enjoy. My first attempt, the fear of losing the social status that I had as an HR Director, led me to accept a job that I had always done and that I had doubts if I enjoyed.

What has helped me in instances where I have overcome fear and followed my passion, is thinking about where the fear comes from. Confronting fear is the best thing you can do in this situation. How do you confront fear? By asking yourself: *What is the worst that will happen should you take steps to follow your passion?*

It's a good idea to do an exercise exploring your fears by writing down a list of the worst that you think might happen as you take those giant steps towards pursuing your passion.

Fear is also aggravated by expectations of our social surroundings. As mentioned in earlier chapters one of the reasons we lose touch with our passion is the influence of our loved ones and our social surroundings. If your family and friends believe you will do well as a doctor, it can be difficult to choose a career that is different to what you have been channelled to by your family. Fear of going against everyone's opinion and only failing might stop you. It's rather safer to follow what everyone is recommending. Think about it, if it doesn't work out no one will say "I told you so."

This, combined with not wanting to disappoint important people in our lives, make us choose careers we know we do not like just to make everyone else happy.

Our social environment can also be a blocker. You might have a dream to follow a specific career aligned to your passion, however, society can have its own expectations and blockers. For example, if you grew up in a society where women's education is seen as less important because women are only expected to get married and become home-makers.

In other societies there tend to be specific careers that are seen as suited to men and women. So if you are in a society where men are expected to occupy masculine roles it might be frowned upon if your passion is to follow a career regarded as feminine such as becoming a social worker as an example. While in Western society this may sound foreign, it is still a reality in other parts of the world. Such social expectations might force us to shy away from following our passion at the beginning of our careers, thus finding ourselves doing jobs that are acceptable to society while remaining unhappy and dissatisfied.

Lack of resources and lack of exposure remain blockers for many others. Imagine growing up in a country where everything is highly controlled by government. Your movements, education, what you could read and write, the job you could do, were all under government scrutiny. Any deviation from what was allowed could cost your and your family's lives. Those were the conditions most of us were born into and under which we spent most of our teenage years as black South Africans during the apartheid regime. Growing up in such an environment, you are bound to have limited educational resources and limited exposure. Most of us chose careers based on the limited knowledge and resources that we had been exposed to.

Furthermore, such an environment instils a "survival mentality" for the generation growing up under these conditions. Survival mentality dictates

– go to school, finish school, find any job so that you are able to provide for your family. The concept of exploring and pursuing your passion is unheard of. The "survival environment" promotes stable and safe careers that are seen as solid and sustainable. For example, being a teacher, a doctor, a nurse were all seen as stable careers. My family would frown upon me coming home declaring that I want to be a painter or a singer. In fact, some parents would even declare: "You need to study so that you can have a real job."

The fact that there might not be role models of successful artists making a living as professional painters in your surroundings is a huge block to you being able to explore a passion in this area. How do you get past a parent who is convinced you need to study something serious so that you can get a "real job"?

As a result, we find ourselves, in jobs we chose in order to comply with social expectations, or to make our loved ones happy or because it was the only career we had resources to pursue. It is no wonder then that in our adult life we have become serial job-hoppers trying to find jobs and work environments that we will enjoy.

The challenge is that once you have chosen a career path and built your career around it, it becomes difficult to change later in life. As you attempt to change careers you encounter financial obstacles which might block you. Money is crucial for our personal survival and in most instances our career decisions are primarily influenced by finances. Successful entrepreneurs and people with fulfilling careers will tell you that if you want to spend your life doing something you love, the best way to start is to treat financial concerns as secondary.

I know this isn't always immediately possible. You might have family members who are dependent on your income, a lifestyle you would like to maintain, or debts that you need to pay off. With these restrictions, you may be wondering how it could be possible to even begin thinking about your passion when so much depends on you bringing in money every week.

Everyone's circumstances will produce a different concern, but the answer to that question lies in knowing how much you really want to live your passion and what you're willing to sacrifice to achieve this. You might have to renounce privileges in the beginning. Your lifestyle may be affected and the luxuries you enjoyed will have to be foregone for the time being. For those with critical responsibilities which cannot be surrendered, such as financially supporting your loved ones, you will require a carefully thought out plan which will allow you to manage your responsibilities while simultaneously pursuing your passion. It'll be harder, but it's not impossible.

Most of us have had blockers to pursuing or even exploring our passion. This is the reason I maintain that your chosen career is a journey. You might be in a job you have ended up doing due to certain circumstances. You should not feel locked to it if you do not like it. There is always a way to unlock yourself and connect with your passion. First you need to be clear what your blockers are and map out a way to unblock yourself and take your big step!

Self-reflection Questions

1. What are your main blockers to exploring and pursuing your passion?

2. What is the source of these blockers?

3. What are you prepared to do to remove these blockers and explore your passion?

4. What action are you committing to take towards removing obstacles to pursuing a career aligned with your passion?

LEARN BEFORE YOU CAN EARN

"What do you need to learn to do what you love?"

Once you have identified what your passion and strengths are, you then need to determine any additional knowledge, skills and experience you need to gather in order to secure a job that fits your passion.

Recent research by educational psychologists O'Keefe, Dweck and Walton indicate that interests and passion alone are not enough to sustain your motivation to build a sustainable career.[10] Interests and passion need to be *developed* once found. Your passion will be revealed to you in a raw state, and it requires your investment in development and growth before it can become the stable foundation for a successful career.

How do you develop your passion?

I often hear people say: "Find out what skills are most in demand in the marketplace and then focus on building those skills."

You *could* do that and maybe you will be marketable, but the question then remains – will you be doing a job that you are passionate about and the one that is aligned to your strengths and talents? The alternative is to consider your passion and strengths first and then plan to build knowledge and skills in demand within your area of passion.

As you take charge of your own development towards a career, focus your efforts on cultivating skills and training in line with your talents, and your passion. Never invest too much time learning something that you have no talent or passion for. Your commitment will falter, and so will your self-esteem. Remember, when you focus on your weaker area, you are doing damage control – minimising the 'damage' caused by your weaknesses. However, that is not development; and it will hold you back from maximising your strengths and talents and reaching your true potential.

In this chapter we discuss ways to build knowledge and skills associated with your talents to prepare yourself for a career aligned with your passion.

For some, this process may start very early in life, but for others it happens later.

For Paul Graham, this process started early. Growing up in Pittsburgh, Pennsylvania in the early 70s, he was fascinated by the depiction of computers in television and film. In junior school he decided to undertake a project on the school computer, an IBM mainframe that was used for printing out grade reports. This was the first time he had gotten his hands on a computer. Over the next few years he taught himself how to program, by consulting the few books that had been written at the time and learning by trial and error. He later decided to study computer science at Cornell University and then went on to Harvard University. Armed with his extensive training, Paul would later develop the first online commerce engine which was bought by Yahoo for $45 million. He didn't stop there; he created *Y Combinator*, an apprenticeship system for young entrepreneurs in technology.

Paul's story brilliantly demonstrates how following your passion from a young age and building knowledge and skills around your passion can enable you to build a successful career *and* to develop a limitless capacity for innovation.

Three Ways to Build Skill and Knowledge in your Areas of Passion

Start with these three key foundations to expand your skill and knowledge base:

1.   Focus on the skills you want to develop

2.   Do your ten thousand hours

3.   Use apprenticeship

Firstly, you must determine the skills and knowledge you will need to build to be successful in your area of passion. Remember from the Ikigai exercise:

Only when what you are good at intersects with what the world needs are you able to trade your skill(s) and get paid for it.

Do your ten thousand hours

Findings from studies conducted in the 1990s by psychologist K. Anders Eriksson guide that ten thousand hours of practice is required to achieve the level of mastery. When I first read this principle in Malcolm Gladwell's book, *Outliers*[11] I was demotivated – ten thousand hours is a lifetime. Gladwell suggests that our ability to achieve excellence in performing a complex task requires a minimum level of practice of ten thousand hours. But then it clicked that we *do* have a lifetime to acquire skills, develop our passion and build a successful career. So it is the ten thousand hours of practice that is required to achieve the level of mastery associated with being world-class – in anything.

Gladwell provides several examples of people who have put in their ten thousand hours and went on to become masters in their field. One of those examples is Bill Joy. Joy stumbled across computer science at the University of Michigan in the early seventies. From that point on he was hooked – the computer centre was his life. He programmed whenever he could. He even secured a job with a computer science professor so that he could program over summer holidays.

In 1975 he enrolled in graduate school at the University of California. There, he buried himself even deeper in the world of computer software. During oral exams for his PhD, he built a particularly complicated algorithm spontaneously which stunned his examiners. Later on, working with a small group of programmers, Joy took on the task of rewriting UNIX, which was the software developed by AT&T for mainframe computers. Joy's version was so good that it became the operating system on which millions of computers around the world ran. Joy also wrote much of the software that allows us to access the internet today.

A number of individuals who are viewed as masters in their chosen careers tell a story of how they used their ten thousand hours to develop their passion and eventually became masters.

Ten thousand hours translates to nine to ten years. This means once you have honed in on your passion, and identified what part of your passion you want to develop, you need to ensure that for the next ten years of your career you focus on practising your trade.

Be an apprentice

Being an apprentice is a phase you enter every time you choose to learn something new, change careers or decide to learn a new skill. Coincidentally Green[5] also believes that the journey towards mastery should take about ten years and begins with apprenticeship. Exploring your trade through apprenticeship works to transform your mind and character to align with your work. During this period your goal is not to acquire a good position, good title, or a qualification – it is to build mastery.

There are three steps to achieving a successful apprenticeship: the 1)Deep Observation step, 2) the Skills Acquisition step, and 3) the Experimentation step.

During the *deep observation* phase your intention is to observe the rules and procedures that guide the success in this particular environment. Some of the rules and procedures will be communicated directly to you and others you have to learn as you get to understand the culture of the environment.

After some months of observation, you enter a period where you begin *acquiring skills*. This can be in a form of learning to use a machine, a system, or organising information. The key to becoming adept at any skill is practice. It helps to focus on one skill that you can acquire which will serve as a foundation for acquiring others.

To accelerate your learning, you begin to independently *experiment* using the learnt skill on your own. This means taking on more responsibility. The purpose of this step is to expose your skill to others and receive feedback to help you address gaps identified.

My first apprenticeship began immediately after qualifying as a social worker. I spent time observing children's court proceedings and shadowing

Alexis, my senior colleague. I also spent months learning about child-care legislation, policies and tools used by the agency's social workers to interview, assess and analyse cases in preparation for court reports. I thought I was ready to start working independently. My first case was that of a kidnapped baby. It involved two women fighting over a baby that they both claimed to be biological parents of. Nothing could have prepared me for that. But the experience was a great way for me to start building confidence to deal with cases on my own.

A key element of your apprenticeship is practising what you're learning by repetition, to acquire and solidify your new skills quickly and accurately. Finding people to learn from who share your interests will help you to understand how they've consolidated their talents, interests, and training into a coherent career path, and how they've moved towards becoming experts in their field. Your apprenticeship phase is the key to learning more about your interests and skills in a practical way which is applicable to the real world.

All of this brings us neatly to our next question: How do you know when you have learnt enough and are ready to start working?

If you are ready to undertake projects on your own, from first conception to implementation and completion, and open yourself up to the scrutiny and feedback of others – then you're ready. As Green[5] suggests, "you will know your apprenticeship is over by feeling that you have nothing left to learn in the area". Pay attention to this feeling!

Finally, developing your passion is a journey that requires patience. It is not true that once you have found your passion you are ready to begin a productive career – that's only the beginning!

Choosing skills you want to learn in support of your passion and focusing on developing that one skill at a time, rather than spreading your time learning multiple skills at once, is more effective. It takes over ten thousand hours of apprenticeship to build a skill to reach mastery level. It is safe to say that developing your passion is a journey intertwined with your career growth.

It requires willingness to put in the hours of practice needed to become confident in your trade. It is not a once-off event of going to college and obtaining a certificate. This is rather a lifelong journey.

Self-reflection Questions

1. My passion that I want to develop more is …

2. Skills I need to learn to pursue my passion are …

3. I will learn this new skill by doing? …

4. To build my expertise I plan to invest my ten thousand hours by …

Step Three

FIND A MENTOR

"Who is the person that inspires you?"

At the age of 33, Becky's career in journalism was thriving. But then she decided she wanted to do something that she genuinely liked. She decided that the first step was to move away from working in a high-paced media job. Becky realised she would need help in order to make this move smoothly and successfully. So she reached out to Joan, a successful estate agent – someone she had admired from afar for some time. She was impressed by how Joan had managed her career and social life, and seemed able to balance her success at work with plenty of time for friends and family.

Becky and Joan started out their relationship with Becky seeking guidance on how to transition from her job as a journalist to something that she always wanted to do – which is running an NGO supporting refugees in crisis. This initial interaction led to a life-long mentoring relationship. According to Becky, "Joan has remained the mentor I never had. Although we have not defined our relationship as that, deep down I know that she plays a valuable mentoring role in my life. She is someone who is always there for me to bounce ideas off, I have learnt a lot from her personal experiences and I find she challenges me to think differently and beyond my comfort zone."

There are many people who can tell a similar story to Becky's – people who have benefited immensely from having a great mentor. Robert Greene[5] reminds us that life is short, and your time for learning and creativity is limited. Without guidance, you can waste valuable years trying to gain knowledge and practical experience from various sources. Instead, follow the example set by masters throughout the ages and find a proper mentor.

A mentor is a person who you look up to, who can be your sounding board. They can provide guidance in times when you need it the most and can challenge you to think about things from a different perspective. He or she is usually someone you respect and who holds a position you aspire to, or is in a field you seek to enter. A mentor is there to share ideas and guide you through your career journey. Typically, mentors share with protégées information about their career path, as well as providing guidance, motivation, emotional support and role modelling. You will find a mentor helpful in exploring careers, setting goals, developing contacts and identifying resources. The mentor role will change as you progress along your path; it is a collaborative relationship.

I appreciate this particular view of a mentor for two reasons. Firstly, it highlights the importance of a mentor as a resource when working on your career. Secondly, it emphasises that the mentorship relationship may change based on your shifting needs and position. The relationship between you and your mentor is based on mutual benefit. You gain from the relationship as much as the mentor benefits. Remember, the relationship with your mentor is a non-reporting one and does not replace any of the organisational structure in your work – it's personal as well as professional.

It's worth noting – as we saw in Becky's case – that while some mentoring relationships begin in an official capacity, others begin unofficially but grow to become mentorship relationships as each party comes to recognise what they can offer to the other. The label and definition are not as important as you finding this supportive structure and knowing how to use it for your benefit. Some of you have had mentors and have found it easy while others might find it difficult and are unsure of where to begin.

If that is the case, then this chapter is for you. In the coming pages, we will focus on the importance of having a mentor when you are defining your career or considering a career change, and we'll unravel the best ways of finding a mentor before we explore how best to use the mentoring set-up.

The importance of having a mentor is closely related to the need to challenge yourself in order to develop your career. A mentor can help at the beginning of your professional life as you define the direction you wish to take. They can help you as you make decisions about changing jobs and companies, as well as offer support should you decide to change or reinvent your career. It can be unsettling to go through such changes on your own, and your confidence can be shaken in the face of new experiences and new fears. You need someone to ground you, someone with whom to share your fears and explore solutions in a safe space, and someone who will help you alter your perspective.

How do you find a suitable mentor?

What are your goals and objectives for the mentoring? If you can answer this question with confidence, you'll be well on the way to finding the perfect mentor.

The starting point for finding your mentor is your existing network of colleagues, previous employers, and the wider professional networks you might have access to through friends or relatives. If a particular person springs to mind right now, you might already know who you want your mentor to be.

What should you look for in a mentor?

Choose a mentor who best fits your needs and connects with your goals. Your choice should be someone you believe you can learn from. A person who can be honest with you and challenge you to think from unfamiliar angles, so you can break through existing thought and behaviour patterns which restrict you.

Unsurprisingly, it's almost impossible to know whether someone is a suitable mentor without having ever met them. Asking a stranger to become your mentor is ill-advised. Sheryl Sandberg, in her book *Lean In*, likens asking strangers to be mentors to the behaviour of the main character in a popular children's book – *Are you My Mother?*. The book is about a baby bird which emerges from its shell in an empty nest and goes around searching for its mother, asking everything it sees "Are you My Mother?". Sheryl Sandberg argues that once you've found the right mentor you do not need to even ask the question. If you have to ask, the answer is probably no.[12]

When someone finds the right mentor, it becomes obvious. The question becomes a statement. Remember, chasing or forcing the mentor connection rarely works.

So your mentor should be someone you know, who is in a position senior to you in your field or industry. It might be someone who is in a career you dream about, and are looking to transition into. I must emphasise that if your focus is to grow and develop within your career, it helps if your mentor is in the same industry as you. This way you can learn and emulate some of the tactics that made *them* successful; and of course, they'll be able to share contacts and training opportunities with you.

Another consideration is whether or not your mentor should work within the same company as you. There are advantages and disadvantages to having a mentor in your company. It can work really well if your goal is to grow within that business – in this instance you can have a mentor and a sponsor. Your mentor can connect you to their networks within the organisation, and they can open doors and break any barriers that you're struggling to manoeuvre through as you work your way up. Your mentor can give you feedback and insight on how you are viewed in the organisation and they will normally look after your interests. I must caution, however, that this works much better in big multinational corporations than in small or local companies. For example, in small businesses you may encounter concerns about favouritism and preferential treatment if you are directly mentored by a senior staff member while other employees are not.

Once you have identified a suitable mentor and are clear on what you want to gain from this relationship, you have taken the first step. You then need to ensure that your mentoring works for you – and that responsibility does lie with you. This requires you to be open about what support you would like from your mentor, and what you want to learn from their experiences. It is good to think about this as you work towards identifying your mentor. But remember that nothing is set in stone; your goals will change and evolve throughout your relationship with your mentor.

How do you make your mentorship work?

There are a number of factors which contribute to a healthy and nourishing mentor relationship. First, you'll need to agree on the frequency of your interaction with your mentor. Remember that you, as the one being mentored, own this process, but it is a collaborative relationship too. It's useful to discuss a frequency that works for both of you, and schedule meetings in advance. Meetings can be face-to-face or conducted online via a platform such as Skype. Due to my ambition to build an international career, I have always had mentors who were based in countries outside of where I lived – I found this gave me invaluable exposure to different ways of thinking and working, and I could draw on the best elements of each mentor's working culture to inform my own professional practice. This was helpful to me when the time came to accept positions outside of my home country, especially as I made a permanent move into the developed markets. Whether you're looking to change cities, countries or continents, interaction with mentors from different backgrounds may prove extremely beneficial in the long run.

Secondly, your mentorship must start with honesty and willingness to be open and vulnerable. Why is this important? Your mentor will be better able to support you if you share your concerns and challenges authentically. I remember a time I was allocated a mentor who was a global executive, because I was on a top talent programme. I went into the mentorship thinking I needed to behave like top talent which, in my mind, meant always being successful. As a result, I was not transparent and open about the challenges I was facing or the fears I was battling. Thinking back, I could have benefited far more from my mentor had I gone in ready to share more openly, rather than trying to impress her. My mentor was only able to guide me based on what I shared with her. This made our mentorship superficial and unhelpful at best, and uncomfortable at worst.

How *do* you know if your mentoring relationship is functioning effectively? You will know it is working if you and your mentor discuss issues important to you and your career. You will have the opportunity to think and reflect after your meetings, and might even have follow-up questions and comments.

Central to all of this though, is that you *take action* as a result of your discussions and the feedback you receive from your mentor. This could be, for example, changing behaviour; taking real-life steps towards your desired career; and updating your mentor on your achievements – big and small – as well as your frustrations and struggles.

It's inevitable that your mentor will, at times, tell you things you don't want to hear. Their job is to challenge you and give you honest feedback. In all honesty, there have been moments in my own mentorships when I've been tempted to end the relationship because I feel confronted or unsettled by their words. But this is not the right time to leave. If you find yourself in this uncomfortable zone, your mentor is doing what they are supposed to be doing: pushing you to change and accelerate your career growth.

Your mentorship will be successful if you use the time together to learn as much as possible from your mentor. He or she went through experiences and learnt lessons which you can learn from as if you'd been through those experiences yourself – you can emulate their successes and avoid repeating their mistakes. In this way, your learning curve is both shorter and smoother.

Mentorship options

Mentors come in all different shapes and sizes. What I mean by this is that a mentor does not necessarily have to be a person you meet face-to-face. Whilst this is most certainly the preferred option, you can find a mentor through training videos, books and online courses.

When finding a mentor, you have the following three options:

Option 1

One-to-one mentoring. Please feel free to contact me at [gugu.khazi@passiontocareers.com] for more information about how I can help you.

Option 2

Career guidance books and training courses. Try How2Become.com for an excellent range of career guidance books and resources.

Option 3

YouTube videos. There are a wide range of fantastic training videos on YouTube to help you prepare for an interview or create a CV. Visit www.YouTube.com/CareerVidz/ for more ideas.

Self-reflection Questions

1. My objective for looking for a mentor is ...

2. I will have had a successful mentorship if my mentor can help me achieve ...

3. I think ... could be a great mentor for me because...

4. I think a mentor can help me achieve my career ambition by ...

5. I will arrange to meet my mentor every (frequency) ...

ESTABLISH YOUR CAREER CHOICES

"What career options do you have?"

By now, you have come face-to-face with your passion. You have begun your learning journey and have begun work to find your ideal mentor. So, it's time to get practical and discover careers that are available for you – with your passion and skills – within your industry of choice.

How can your unique interests and experience provide value? Note that I intentionally have not spoken about finding a job, but rather a career and value. The reason for this is that as soon as you start looking for a *job* you will go back to packaging yourself to suit someone else's expectations without considering your interests. If you take that approach, the journey is no longer about you, but rather about the company and the job requirements. In this chapter we will focus on what you must consider when making your career choice.

You want to keep your exploration about you and your talents as well as the value that you can create using your interests, strengths and passion. When you look at available careers you are exploring: What do people with your interests and passion do and in which industry do they tend to work?

It's normal to explore career choices several times during your journey. As you plan and prioritise your studies in school or university, you are confronted with the question of what career you want to pursue. As you start working, you often have to ask yourself again what choices you have, based on what you have studied. You constantly have to ask yourself about your career choices as you change jobs, change companies, and consider reinventing your career.

Multiple factors come into play when you make a career choice. You have to think about your studies, and what attracted you to your studies. Another factor is industry; you need to consider what industries are your first choice to work in and are there any industries which are absolutely not for you?

Kevin, my mentee, was quite clear that he liked working for development agencies which he perceived to have a positive impact on people's lives. He was very passionate about development in underdeveloped countries and his dream was to find a job that would post him in a community development job in a developing country. He was also very clear about specific industries he would not work in, including the tobacco and arms industries. This gave him his foundation of values from which to build a career.

Consider the industry

It's likely that there are multiple industries that could use your passion. For me, knowing that I like working with people and having a positive impact on their lives could propel me into a number of sectors – including social services and corporate industries. And the number of choices available to me have, indeed, caused my professional life to date to be very varied. I've worked in airports, oil and gas, banking, and consumer goods industries, always with the common thread that my role was people-focused.

One common mistake is to limit yourself to careers and industries that already exist. That means defining your personal value by the standards of others. In this day and age, there are innumerable opportunities to create new value and craft a new career for yourself. As economies and technology evolve, new industries are being established. Existing industries are being disrupted and new careers are emerging. Just look at new businesses like Uber, Airbnb, and all the sharing-based and collaborative consumption businesses that have emerged.

By focusing on *you*, your strengths and your interests and the value you can bring to the market, you can look at careers and industries that already exist, study how they view and create value and redefine the value for the industry. There are multiple examples from the emerging new technologies. The emerging e-commerce industry provides a great opportunity for you to reshape old industries and create a new and innovative market. What I am emphasising here is that you should not be afraid to explore new upcoming industries; that is where you will find the most learning.

Consider location

Don't let the geographical location of your career be an afterthought. Where are most of the jobs available within your chosen career based? Could you work from anywhere, or would you be expected to tie yourself to a specific place?

For example, if you choose the financial sector, you will most likely thrive in London – the financial capital of the United Kingdom and the acclaimed financial capital of the world. While it's easy to disregard geography during your career decision-making process, it's vitally important. Whether or not you are willing to relocate, to travel, or *not* to travel has a significant impact on the work available to you.

Most industries are in clusters. This is a common phenomenon where firms from the same industry gather together in one location. For example, in the United Kingdom the financial sector is clustered in London, while the high-tech cluster is growing in Bristol. These examples are applicable in the UK but think of yourself and your country and where the industries related to your career are clustered. And then ask yourself: Are you willing to relocate there?

Yes, there are opportunities to work remotely and be part of virtual teams. However, I have observed that companies are happy to have virtual teams for junior roles, but when it comes to senior roles there might be less flexibility for remote work.

Geography plays a part in the jobs available to you, and also gives you a head start in understanding where you should focus your career search.

Consider company values and ethics

Moving into even greater detail, it's important to consider the company you want to work for itself and explore factors that will contribute to whether or not you'll enjoy working there. Big businesses often have a persona and a reputation of their own, created by the values and behaviours that the leaders promote. Does your chosen company reflect your values back at you in the products they sell, the way they do business, and how they treat their customers and employees? It's disconcertingly common to ignore these questions when we're looking for a job. We focus on what the job is and what it offers in terms of day-to-day life and pay. As more companies are engulfed by scandal after scandal, ethics and corporate governance is taking centre stage. Your career choice should take issues of ethics and values seriously, both when choosing your industry of choice and your company of choice. It does not help you to choose a big company that is doing well but is continuously involved in malpractice or which does not care about the key social issues that are important to you.

Consider the job itself

How do you know if a job presented to you will fulfil and inspire you? The rule of thumb I encourage my clients to use is that 60% of what the job requires should involve things you like doing. Sounds simple – but keeping this rule in mind will help you make the right choices and avoid jumping into a new professional role for the wrong reasons. Remember, you will be spending around 60% of your day, five days a week doing this job. So why not make it interesting?

There are several techniques you can use to establish what percentage of the job is linked to your passion. The go-to technique for many of us is to read through the job description, highlighting the key requirements and expectations of the job. This has limitations because a lot can be hidden in a job description, or left out entirely.

Another valuable method for confirming if the job content is aligned with your passion is to speak to the team leader who advertised the job. This is an important step which most people ignore. The way a job is described on paper might be quite different to the daily reality of that role. So, to avoid later disappointment, speak to the team leader about what a day in the role might look like, and what specific tasks, responsibilities and expectations are attached to it. If the company is hiring in order to replace a member of staff who is leaving, find out what that person actually does day to day. Now, how realistic is it that you will be able to access the team leader of a job that is being advertised by recruitment agencies? Actually, if you ask, you'll more than likely be offered a phone call. Employers are interested in hiring people who are interested in them – and asking to speak with your potential team leader in order to ascertain whether a job is right for you or not shows that you are interested and proactive.

The third effective way of establishing if the job is really a good fit for your needs is to speak to individuals who are already doing the job at the same company. As mentioned, the person you're replacing may be the most valuable person to speak to; but if you can't connect with them – or if the role isn't being advertised to replace someone at all – then other employees at a similar level within the company are worth chatting with. Remember, job titles can be uniform across different companies, but the way that job is done might be completely different from one company to the next; so it is useful to get a specific view of that position in that company.

The industry in which you work, location of the company you work for, and the ethics and values of the company you choose to work for are key factors that can impact how your career develops. It is important that you pay as much attention to these factors as you would to the job itself.

Self-reflection Questions

1. My ideal industry to work in is …

2. The locations ideal for my long-term career are …

3. The values and ethical considerations important for me in a potential employer or company are …

4. The key characteristics that make a job exciting to me are …

BE READY TO INTERVIEW

"Do you belong in this place?"

Up to this point we have looked at you preparing yourself to be interviewed. That means preparing to answer someone else's questions about how good you are and what value you can add to their business. Now, however, it's time to consider how to prepare yourself for your interview from a you-centric perspective – how to use your interview to glean the details you need to discover about the job and discern whether or not it's a good fit for you.

This approach is a bit different, as it is *you* who is preparing to interview your potential employer. Yes, you will still need to show that you meet the job requirements and demonstrate your worthiness for the role. But simultaneously, it's vital to know by the end of an interview, whether the job meets your personal interests and what percentage of the job is aligned to your passion.

Just as employers prepare for interviews, you will also need to prepare to interview the company. In this chapter we will look at how to ready yourself for an interview. We'll cover key questions to ask your interviewers in order to determine whether you want to accept the job should it be offered to you.

During an interview, an employer will ask questions about you focusing on your skills, experience, performance, track record and sometimes educational achievement with the intention of deciding whether you meet the company requirements. You must ask questions about the role, growth opportunities, and company culture, with the intention of deciding whether this is a position which will match your interests, talents and passion.

Don't waste your time exploring jobs which have no connection to your interests. I understand that you might be in a state of survival and need a job to make ends meet, but the fact is that once you start compromising on your interests it becomes a pattern – and could end up defining the rest of your career. Take a deep breath and take your time.

After establishing that the job offers elements in line with your talents and interests, you then need to be able to sell your passion and interests to the company. Note that you are not only selling your skills, knowledge or experience as is traditionally the case – you are selling your passion.

How do companies interview?

Many employers use the *Competency Based Interviewing* approach which sets out to ascertain whether an interviewee's competencies and skills meet the job requirements. This interviewing technique allows them to probe your knowledge and experience in a particular job. They will ask you to tell a story about how you have dealt with a particular situation. The principle of this interviewing technique is that past performance and behaviour predicts future performance and behaviour. In other words, what you have done in the past is a predictor of what you will do in the future and how you will perform in the job. The questions are behaviour-based and focus on the traits and skills deemed necessary for succeeding in a job or an organisation.

The questions are framed in a way that requires you to reflect on your past performance, and they focus on your behaviours. Such questions often begin with: "Tell me about a time when…," "Describe a time when you…," or "Give me an example of a time when…"

For example, an interviewer for a job which involves lots of customer service would invariably ask: "Tell me about a time when you had to deal with an irate customer."

Each candidate is asked the same questions so that the quality of the answers can be directly compared. What does this mean for you? You need your answers to be the best of the bunch. And you can achieve that by mastering the art of storytelling.

Don't worry – I have a simple technique to help you perfect your storytelling, every single time. The STAR technique asks you to consider:

- Situation: Your story must describe the situation that you had to deal with relevant to the question you've been asked.

- Task: It must give detail of the task you were expected to perform.

- Action: Your story must demonstrate that you took positive action to negotiate the situation.

- Results: Your story concludes with an outcome which shows that your actions were appropriate or that you learnt a valuable lesson from the situation which you will carry with you into future encounters.

So, to use the example of dealing with an irate customer, you could answer:

Situation: *While working at ABC Company I once had a customer return her purchase because the product had an incorrect size label, but the problem was she was returning it after the allowable return date.*

Task: *My role was to record the returned products and refund customers.*

Action: *On seeing how angry she was and realising the risk to the company, even though the policy said she was not allowed to return the product, I reached out to my manager, explained the situation and suggested that because the incorrect label was our fault, we should allow her to be refunded.*

Result: *My manager agreed and I refunded her, and we had a happy customer, who went on to buy more products in the shop.*

The above example is simplified to give you a sense of how the STAR technique might work in real terms.

Typical behavioural questions that you may be asked could focus on a time that you:

1. Worked effectively under pressure.
2. Handled a difficult situation with a co-worker.
3. Were creative in solving a problem.
4. Missed an obvious solution to a problem.
5. Were unable to complete a project on time.

The best way to prepare for interviews is to identify required competencies listed in the job description, and practise with some questions and answers using the above technique.

Now your turn to ask questions

Once you've answered the interviewer's questions and sold your passion and interests, it's your turn to ask questions and determine if the job on offer meets any of your passions. Your questions will start by establishing what type of person will be successful in the job. This drives the conversation to look beyond skills and experience, to the person that the company sees as possessing characteristics that will make them successful in the job. You can ask the question in a number of ways, such as: "For me to be successful, what characteristics do I need to have?" or "What characteristics should the incumbent have for them to be successful in this job?" During the discussion that ensues, take note of the characteristics which are emphasised and the reasons they are seen as important.

You also need to get to the best possible sense of how much time you will spend doing work that is aligned with your passion. In the interview you can phrase it as a question gauging what you will be doing on a daily/weekly/monthly basis. For example: "Can you describe a typical day/week/month in this job?" or "As well as the tasks listed in the job description, what other tasks or errands will I be expected to undertake each day?" Your interviewer's answers to these questions should help to paint a picture of what the job is really like, in real terms.

Once you have established that the job on offer is aligned with your interests, you can broach the issue of how much – if any – potential the role holds for growth within your career. You can be really direct about this; employers tend to appreciate candidates who express a firm desire to progress within the company. So, you could ask, for example: "What growth opportunities does your company provide for someone with a strong passion for numbers and analysis like me?" The answer to this question will help you determine if you will be able to grow in your areas of interest within this company. Look out for vague and non-committal answers like "You can grow as much as you want as an individual, it is up to you." An answer like this should ring alarm bells. You might want to follow up with another question like: "While I fully agree with taking ownership of my career growth, what support does this company provide to help me move forward?" If your interviewer is unable to answer this question with reassurance, the company is unlikely to be prepared to support your development in a structured and definitive way.

Always focus on the culture

All the above should be followed by questions regarding the company culture. Are you wondering what company culture has to do with whether a job is aligned to your passion and interests? Well – it has everything to do with it. A company's culture tells you how things are done and whether internal interactions are positive and supportive, or competitive and conflict-based. What is valued, and what is rewarded. Leadership author and founder of the Barrett values centre, Richard Barrett[14] suggests that the culture of an organisation reflects the values and beliefs of the current leaders that are embedded in the structures, policies, systems, procedures and incentives of the company.

Depending on what the company culture is like, some interests and passions will thrive while others will not. Take, for example, a company that values the retention of old ways of doing things and puts controls in place to ensure compliance to these. Such a company will not value or reward an individual who is passionate about finding new and innovative techniques or creating and updating systems. This doesn't mean the company is bad, but it does mean that if you like change, starting something new and doing things differently, then this company is not for you. You will not thrive. You will be frustrated, and you're less likely to be successful in your job.

In the table below you'll find a breakdown of typical company cultures which you might encounter on your career journey, and the type of interests and passions which thrive in these cultures.

Culture	Interest/passion
Clan-oriented Culture – family-like cultures with a focus on monitoring, nurturing and doing things together.	Suited to those who are passionate about growing and developing, and about teamwork and cooperation.
Adhocracy-oriented culture – dynamic and entrepreneurial with focus on risk-taking, innovation and doing things first.	Suited to those with passion for starting new things, changing ways of working, and with the entrepreneurs' spirit.
Market-oriented cultures – results-oriented, with focus on competition, achievement and getting the job done.	Suited to those who are passionate about results, want to beat competition and aren't afraid of confrontation, and thrive on high achievement and praise.
Hierarchy-oriented culture – structured and controlled with a focus on efficiency, stability and doing things right.	Suited to those who are passionate about functional and logical processes, who enjoy working in a structured environment and prefer to know what to expect each day.

(Adapted from Robert E, Quinn and Kim S. Cameron, Michigan University)[13]

Remember that no culture is better than another; it all depends on what the company is trying to achieve and how *you* fit into that. Not all cultures will be suited to all your passions, and some will be stifling to your passion. For example, if you like start-ups, innovation and creating new things, you will not do well in a hierarchy-oriented culture, but you will thrive in an adhocracy culture. I have provided you with a culture questionnaire on pages 131 to 135 in the tool kit. Use it to determine your preferred work culture.

Megan is a high-performing marketing professional. She is results-driven and likes working in a fast-paced environment. She had been working for her first employer for over five years and believed that she needed to gain experience in a different company in order to grow her career. When she was offered a job as a marketing manager at another company, she thought her dreams had come true. Her new employer was a well-known company with thriving brands in the cosmetics industry. Megan expected the culture to be the same as in her previous job – but after being in the company for five months she realised she'd made a mistake. As an independent professional who preferred to work in a fast-paced environment and get things done, she could not deal with the slow-paced way of working at her new company. Moreover, she found that she was expected to involve a lot of people in the process of decision making which slowed everything down even more. She felt as though her ideas were stifled by people who made decisions on projects that they knew little about, or cared little about. By the sixth month, Megan had reached out to her previous employer and had come to an agreement to return to the job she'd left.

To avoid making the same mistake as Megan, take time to think about the types of culture to which your talent and passion will be most suited. Also remember that you might have a combination of cultures in an organisation. So, as you prepare to interview your potential employers, keep in mind questions which can get to the bottom of a company's culture.

I often advise my clients to prepare an *interview kit*. In your kit your will have a career story, which covers where you have worked, what your key successes were in each job, what you learnt in that job, and why you left. The kit also has your rehearsed STAR answers to commonly asked competency-based questions as discussed above. Lastly, the kit has key questions to ask your potential employer to determine if this is the right job for you.

Self-reflection Questions

1. What I will do to prepare for my interviews is ...

2. The main questions I will ask my interviewers are...

3. These questions are important because ...

4. Based on the culture assessment, the type of company culture I prefer to work in is ...

GROW YOUR PASSIONS

"Never stop learning."

To grow and nurture your passion is to deepen your knowledge and experience in your field. Growing your passion means you acquire new knowledge, skills and experience that will push you forward and stretch you into new places. In this chapter we explore ways to nurture and build your passion throughout your career.

The 2018 Deloitte Annual Human Capital Trends report shows that the 3rd most important trend emerging in companies is the 21st century career, which is a different approach to career development. Instead of upward career moves, the focus is now on a series of developmental experiences, each offering you the opportunity to acquire skills, exposure and build your track record.[14]

Growing your career involves creating a path on which you will learn new skills, gain new knowledge, and encounter new experiences which help you move towards achieving your career goals. Note that career paths are no longer about moving up the career ladder, but instead about acquiring the right knowledge and experiences to achieve a specific career goal you have set for yourself.

As your career is made up of multiple jobs, each job you take contributes to your learning and provides you with greater experience which hopefully moves you towards achieving your next career milestone. Therefore, as you change jobs, keep in mind where you want to take your career. What is the next job that you want to do, and what skills are required for that job?

Think one step ahead. As soon as you find a job, keep in the back of your mind the *next* job that you are preparing yourself for. In order to do this effectively, you need a career plan.

Plan your career growth

Vital to planning your career growth is knowing, with clarity, what you're aiming for. Where do you want to take your career? What do you want to achieve – or what position do you eventually want to reach? Knowing this allows you to plan a coherent path which will enable you to gain the necessary skills and experience to get where you want to go.

Think about where you'd like to be in five or ten years. Having this vision will help you tailor your journey to the career you want, and set you on the path to success.

Of course, for many of us it's difficult to plan – or even imagine – that far ahead. This is normal and it shouldn't discourage you because what is important is to know what comes after your current job, or even the next two jobs. Where will you thrive? What will make you feel that delicious rush of achievement?

A career plan is helpful because it defines your development. It tells you what skills and experience you need to acquire in order to reach your next career milestone. This will make it easier to decide on the next jobs you must take. Your career masterplan should outline:

- The experience, knowledge and skill you need to acquire or enhance.
- What jobs will provide the best opportunity to acquire this experience.
- The industry or company that is best positioned to provide you with this experience.

I have provided you with a careers master plan template on pages 138 to 139 of the toolkit. Once your plan is in place, you're ready to apply the following techniques to grow your career.

Continuously build your skills and capabilities

It is important to have a skill or trade that you are continuously building. As the world of business changes, the skills that are in demand are also changing. You need to keep track of how this change is impacting your industry and your profession. For example, if you are a recruiter, your job has changed significantly over the past ten years; technology has brought various changes that you have had to learn to use to source and engage candidates. The increasing internal recruitment focus by companies has meant that if you are working in a recruitment agency you define your value proposition differently to remain relevant to your customer needs.

While this is applicable to a person in a recruitment career, this kind of change can be seen in most jobs. Most industries are affected by availability of improved technology and automation. Similarly, most jobs are affected by other massive industry changes. Growing your career is all about keeping track of potential changes influencing your industry and responding by adapting and expanding your skill set. This is echoed by *The Report on Navigating the Future of Work* commissioned by Deloitte which concluded that individuals will need to take greater responsibility for acquiring and continuously updating skills to keep in touch with relevant labour market development[15]

Find a way to differentiate yourself

Acquiring a new skill is a powerful method for differentiating yourself from your competitors. Personally, I am currently learning digital and e-commerce tools to add to my repertoire. Although I am in a Human Resources job, I'm conscious of the fact that in the future understanding social media and being able to position my professional services on a range of online platforms will be critical for my field of work.

The process of differentiating yourself will never end. Over time, your colleagues will catch up with you and you'll be running with the pack again. This is why you need to perpetually generate ways of differentiating yourself, accumulating new skills and enriching your offerings with new experiences.

Back to school

There are a number of examples for how you can break out from the pack. Sometimes going back to school and obtaining a qualification is an effective way of setting yourself apart. More so if you are in a profession which requires professional qualifications and continuing education. There is nothing as refreshing and refocusing as taking a break from work and spending time at university, before coming back to continue with your career. It provides you with an opportunity to clarify whether you really still want to do the work that you do – whether it is really your passion. And there's the added benefit of bringing back new knowledge and new ways of working.

Take a detour

Besides going back to school, you could take a detour and work in a different department – preferably a department that you work closely with in your job, or one that has a strong influence on your area of specialisation.

Take Ralph, for example. He had been in the marketing department of his company for six years when he decided to take a detour and join the finance team for a two-year assignment. After spending two years learning how things are done in finance, he went back to his job in the marketing department, having developed new analytical skills. These newly acquired skills allowed him to build capability *and* credibility, as he can now speak with authority on matters relating to finance with his colleagues. This sets him apart from others on the marketing team which, in the long run, makes him a more viable candidate for progression and promotion.

Overseas experience

My first overseas experience was an eye opener. I was nominated to be part of a mergers and acquisitions team that was bidding for business in India. My role was to conduct due diligence on how a company we were interested in acquiring managed their human resources. This was easy and exciting, I thought – being confident in my solid HR capability. I was going to get there, I knew exactly what questions to ask in line with my experience and I was confident I would produce a brilliant report.

It wasn't until I arrived in Mumbai and started looking at the company's employee benefits that I realised I was out of my depth on this project. I had never seen any of the benefits that were offered, and the complexity involved was way beyond my experience. Needless to say, my attempt to write a meaningful report within the required timeline was a major challenge. However this experience is one that I count among the greatest exposures in my career.

Gaining overseas experience gives you an alternative perspective on your professional life and the working world in general. You might take a break to study abroad or seek work opportunities on unfamiliar soil. This exposure will teach you, on the ground, how other places and people do things. You'll learn about cultures different from your own, and you will go through character-building experiences which are appreciated by all potential employers. This kind of developmental experience is priceless for almost all fields of work.

Getting personal: How I crafted my career growth

After studying social work and working as a social worker for two years, I realised my passion was about helping people but in a different way. I wanted to help people increase their productivity and fulfilment at work. So, I moved to running a recruitment desk in an agency. I enrolled for my Masters in Business specialising in strategic management while in my HR jobs. That was a great differentiator for my next jobs in HR. It helped me in two ways: One, I was able to move up to the next levels in my job, becoming an HR manager. And two, it allowed me to work in various areas of HR due to my understanding of business strategy. As a result, I was able to move around different areas within HR acquiring all the experience needed to move up to a Director role. I always aspired to work in an international environment, and as a result, I ensured that companies I worked for were multinational. I further took a sabbatical to study at an overseas university, which provided me with great international exposure. It was while I was studying that I was approached by a multinational company which opened doors to a number of international roles that I've undertaken since.

Throughout my career I've made sure that my manager is aware of my next career aspirations. And I have found that because my bosses have known where I aspired to go, they've always matched me with the opportunities I needed. I prefer having a conversation with my boss about my career. The last career conversation I had with my boss went exactly like this: "I'm still enjoying my job, my mission in the next year is to fix South African HR and get us to be rated top ten of the top employers. After that I will be ready for a move. I would still like to grow within Kimberly-Clark, and I will appreciate your guidance on how we can make this happen." I drove the conversation and got him to start thinking about my next move long before I needed to move. Within a year I achieved my goal and an opportunity became available to move to a new role. If an opportunity had not become available internally, I would have looked for other opportunities outside of the company.

Why you should not rely on your employer to grow your career

Most companies offer learning and development opportunities to their employees. This is valuable and you should always take advantage of the learning opportunities provided by your employer. However, never rely solely on your employer to progress your skill-set and career because they will invariably focus on honing the skills required by your current job. Make use of these opportunities but always search for external experiences too. This will help you keep up with new trends and technologies, and remain competitive within your field.

Self-reflection Questions

1. My five-year career master plan is ...

2. My next career move is going to be ...

3. The strategies I will adopt to grow my career are...

4. This is what I will do to create unique experiences to grow my career ...

REINVENT YOUR PASSION

"Continuously evolve."

"Authentic being is what we call 'vocation'. But the majority of men devote themselves to silencing that voice of the vocation and refusing to hear it. They manage to make a noise within themselves ... to distract their own attention in order not to hear it; and they defraud themselves by substituting for their genuine selves a false course of life."

– Jose Ortega Gasset

Whether you subscribe to the idea that we all have a predetermined vocation or not, it is evident is that some of us reach a point in our career where we realise that it is not fulfilling for us. We realise that we've had to silence our true passions in a quest to build a traditional career, or because we needed to comply with the expectations of others. Equally, the conditions we find ourselves in as we grow up can affect what inspires us and how able we are to pursue our passions. My initial passion was as a result of the terrible apartheid conditions I lived under. I became fixated with helping others due to the poverty I observed and was part of when I was growing up. I believed that becoming a social worker would allow me to give back to the society that had taken care of me. I'm still passionate about helping others today but my passion has now shifted – to helping others realise their true potential, rather than helping them with basic survival. To follow my new passion required me to reinvent my career.

Reinventing your career provides you with an opportunity to rethink who you are, what your key strengths are and how you want to use your strengths and passions to contribute to society. Most of us started our careers believing we had a passion for a particular area, but later discovered other, and perhaps more potent passions.

There are many reasons you might find yourself considering to reinvent your career. For some, reinvention comes after confronting the realisation that their existing career grew from circumstance, social conditioning or misplaced expectations, rather than passion. Others, like myself, pursue a career aligned to their passion but at a later stage realise they would like to use their passion in a different way. They still remain in the same passion area – what changes is how they express their passion. I have also heard of those who grow up certain of their passion, only to find that it evolves and changes with age. They realise they no longer enjoy what they do.

Whatever the reason, when you get to the point where you realise you need a career change it is difficult to stop or delay it. It's akin to staying in an unhappy relationship after you realise it's not working anymore – the change is inevitable and there's no going back after those doubts have crystallised into clarity. This chapter contains guidance on how to manage your transition to a career you love.

Interestingly, many of us keep working in jobs we no longer enjoy for some time, up until a trigger forces us to re-evaluate. Triggers come in many forms. For me it was not being recognised for extreme hard work, after having spent a year building a new department. I worked myself into the ground that year creating a new team, building processes, and implementing new working practices and communication avenues. When the time came for end-of-year performance reviews, my rating was lower than 100%. I was extremely disappointed and felt hurt by this at the time. Today, I am grateful for the experience because it was my trigger to re-evaluate what was important to me, what my passion was and if I was using my potential to full capacity. This trigger was the catalyst for me to focus on nurturing and growing my areas of passion. I started writing and speaking more in forums, sharing what I know with others.

My experience is aligned to a common belief that you only reinvent yourself after experiencing a major setback. While disappointment and loss do create ideal conditions for reinvention, I urge you to open up to the possibility of reinventing yourself periodically, without waiting to be prompted by major setbacks in life. Tom's transition, which I'll share with you now, is a good example of a transition that came naturally without a specific trigger.

What does reinventing your career involve?

Tom graduated from college in 1965 with an English degree. After graduating he took a job in an insurance company, where he worked for seven years, and soon after he moved into an insurance agency where he worked for another eight years. In 1980, he decided to buy a small insurance agency. At this point Tom had been working in the insurance industry for 15 years, but he was beginning to feel an internal pull to do work that really excited him. He had *always* wanted to write a novel. He started writing in his spare time, then he started cutting his workday short so that he would have more time to write. Eventually, he was working on his writing whenever he could find time. His wife, Wanda, recalls Toms early writing years by saying, "He was writing at home every weekend. I told him he should go back to selling insurance." In 1984, after working almost 20 years in the insurance industry, Tom Clancy finally published his first book, *The Hunt for Red October*. He was hoping to sell 5000 copies but he went on to sell two million copies in ten years, and became one of the most successful writers of his generation.

Tom's story demonstrates how we can find ourselves in a career or job that we've stuck with for decades but which is not aligned with our passion. We might have found the job enjoyable initially, or perhaps it did suit our interests and goals earlier in life. However, after spending a considerable amount of time doing it, we find ourselves with an urge to do something else. Something completely different. Can you relate to that? If you answer yes, then you may be approaching self-reinvention.

Reinventing yourself is not easy. It's not something you wake up in the morning and decide to do. It takes time and understanding of yourself, as well as of your new – or dormant – passion. Most people will realise they do not enjoy what they're doing anymore and will discover their new exciting passion but will end it there because the process of reinventing yourself and transitioning into a new career can feel incredibly scary. But it need not be scary. There are tried and tested ways to successfully reinvent your career; and in this chapter I share those strategies with you.

The majority of people who have gone through career transitions speak of similar steps they had to take. Invariably, it starts with the realisation that you desire change because you're dissatisfied with your current situation.

Now, the easiest thing to do is to change companies, hoping to find something different on the other side. But when people do this they get to the other side and all too often experience the same dissatisfaction. And so they try to change jobs again. The unintended outcome is a CV with a long list of employers, with an average of six to twelve months spent in each role. While there are some advantages of job-hopping within certain industries, the general consensus among employers is that it doesn't prove a reliable track record, or build transferable skills and in-depth experience. Changing jobs thoughtlessly and without a clear vision to address your career dissatisfaction does not lead to any major change – in fact, it's more likely to lead to major frustration later on.

Only by reinventing your career will you change the way you feel. Those that have gone through a process of reinventing themselves explain that interim changes, like finding a new employer, only address the dissatisfaction for a short period before it creeps back in. Do not be tempted by a short-term solution.

And equally, do not allow fear to hold you back. Anxiety about trying something new can be debilitating. The biggest fear for many of us is the fear of failing. But what helps me all the time is to ask myself the question: "So what is the worst that can happen if I fail? Will someone die?" – and every day the answer is NO. So I keep pushing towards my dreams.

How can you reinvent your career successfully?

You've come to the realisation that you want to reinvent your career. So start taking action. This doesn't mean that you immediately drop everything you're doing and pursue something new, but it does mean taking your first steps while still doing your current job. I started out by waking up an hour earlier every morning to write a chapter in my book before going to work.

I suggest that you spend time on weekends learning a new skill. It surely takes you out of your comfort zone and prepares you for what is to come. By starting with little actions towards your journey, you begin to attract the right people and relevant resources to create momentum for your new journey.

One element common to all those who have reinvented themselves is a willingness to make sacrifices – to give up something that was previously important to them. In the beginning you might need to give up your time, your weekends, your sleep, or your holidays. I'm currently giving up my sleep and my weekends, waking up early in the morning to spend an hour writing and the same on weekends. The amazing thing I have discovered while doing this is that it is not difficult, and it doesn't feel like something that I have to force myself to do. Why? Because I'm following my passion, so motivation and inspiration come easily. In the words of Steve Harvey, "I don't care what you do, you've got to give up something to get to the next level."

It helps to learn from those who have travelled the path before you. Identify what worked for them, learn from their mistakes, and choose a path that aligns with your strengths. There is no perfect way to manage your career change. But the recommended approaches can help you to create your own, personally suited method.

The plan and implement vs testing and learning approach

There are two opposing views on how a successful transition comes about. One view maintains that planning, followed by implementation, is the key to success – so the better the plan the smoother the transition. The "plan and implement" approach suggests that before you transition into a new career you can analyse yourself, then plan based on the outcome of your self-assessments to determine what you like or what interests you. This is then followed by you implementing a well-created plan.

However, empirical studies show that it is not realistic to plan yourself into a new future. Rather, career transition involves "testing and learning"[16] Based on her research in this field, Hermina Ibarra[16] found that we learn by taking action one step at a time and responding to the outcomes of the actions we take. This approach confirms that no matter how much planning you do, you still need to *just start taking action*, so you can see the outcomes of your actions and respond to those outcomes. The implementation of a ready-made linear plan is ineffective because it has to change depending on what you learn along the way. In fact, it is not possible to think up a thorough plan to implement. It is only once you begin taking little steps towards your reinvention that you begin testing the possible futures.

Naturally as you explore your various possible futures, you will find yourself going through a phase of confusion. You will encounter chaos and experience feelings of uncertainty. Don't worry – this is normal and healthy. It allows you to think and configure a number of possibilities and explore different opportunities until you settle on the opportunity that best suits your passion. Typically, in this phase you have started taking action towards your new career but you're still engaged in your current career.

The risk at this stage is temptation to hold on too dearly to your existing job and lifestyle. The opposite risk, of course, is of jumping into a new career too fast. Balance is key: Find that sweet spot between holding on and jumping off the edge; a spot in which you feel calm, in control, and full of excitement for what's to come.

Coincidentally, this is exactly the stage I'm in at the moment. I've been working in the Human Resources field for over 19 years – and I've recently accepted that this career is not my passion anymore. So, I've started taking action to propel me towards a new path. I am in that in-between place, still holding onto my old job but also acting on my possible career possibilities. While I have started taking action towards the field of work that I am passionate about, it's not yet clear exactly what it will look like when I have fully transitioned into my new career. The transition phase is very uncomfortable, especially if you are someone who favours planning and stability over the unknown. You cannot predict the outcomes of your new journey. So, if you find yourself feeling this way, know that you are on the right track; do not be scared by the feeling of confusion and uncertainty of this stage.

This view is supported by Joi Ito, Director of MIT Meia Lab, who believes in the principle of *compass over maps*. A good compass will always take you where you need to go. While you might not have a complete career map, with a compass you will always be guided in the right direction.

A little dissatisfaction is okay

As human beings we have more talents than we'll ever have opportunity to explore. Large parts of our working personalities will have to go to the grave without being explored. This is because it is humanly impossible for us to do multiple jobs and fulfil all of our passion areas. Society is structured such that we specialise in just a small area. If everyone does everything, only a small number of shoes, houses, computers, phones, and cars will ever be produced and no one will be especially good at anything. We all have at least nine other employable selves – there is no way we can exercise all of them. It is important to identify the most prevalent one, the one that has the most connection with your passion and inner self, and focus on it. This means we have to accept that some aspects of ourselves will feel dissatisfied at times because there will always be underused talents bubbling beneath the surface of our lives.

A little dissatisfaction with your career and the job you do is normal. However, when it takes over and dissatisfaction overrides the feelings of fulfilment, you need to broach the subject of a career transition. In spite of the impossibility of planning every step of your journey, you can create some security for yourself by following guidelines and actionable advice along the way. Just be aware that it's unlikely that you'll go through the transition exactly as you plan to. Taking action and learning from the outcomes of your actions leads you to deal with the reality of a transition process.

So, do your self-assessment to confirm what your talents, strengths and passions are. Do the transition plan but ensure that you act on your plans.

Learn from the outcomes and adjust your plans as you go along. Be mindful that you cannot explore all your talents, and you will always experience some small level of dissatisfaction regardless of the route you take. That's a good thing – it can remind you of the infinite potential that exists within your consciousness.

Self-reflection Questions

1. The top 5 reasons I want to reinvent my career are...

2. The first steps I will take towards reinventing my career are ...

3. Potential blockers I might encounter as I go through reinventing my career are ...

4. My role model as I go through this transition is ...

ALWAYS LEAVE A LEGACY

"How to create habits of success."

"Carve your name on hearts not on stones, a legacy is stetted into the minds of others and the stories they share about you" – Shannon L Alders

When I started working for one particular employer, I found an interesting incentive system. The system provided a way of calculating individual performance bonuses based on company performance. The intriguing thing about this system was that you either liked it or loathed it – there was no in-between. It was called the "Don's system". When I did further investigation into why it went by that name, I discovered that a gentleman called Don Roberts had created the system. Don had long left the company, but his legacy remained. This is what I call tangible legacy – creating products or processes that change ways of doing things and have an impact long after you have left.

On the contrary, when I joined Kimberly-Clark, one of the people I had already heard about was the Managing Director who was known for knowing and remembering the names of every single person in the organisation. Not only did Garth know everyone's name, he also knew – and was genuinely interested in – each person's story. He remembered whose child was due to go to college, whose mom was in hospital and who was going through a tough time. Even after Garth had left the organisation, stories about how well he knew everyone and how he interacted with people still remained. Garth left what I call an intangible emotive legacy; he had such a positive impact on the people he came into contact with that he would not be forgotten.

These two forms of legacy have equal value. Neither is better than the other. What is important is to realise that your work within a company has the potential to create a legacy that you will be remembered for – or you will be known for nothing. As you build your career track record, you want to leave a positive legacy in each organisation that you work within. This chapter discusses the importance of legacy and a number of ways to cultivate that legacy throughout your career.

What is a legacy?

There is a common belief that you should start thinking about what kind of legacy you want to leave when you reach the age of 50, up to about 60, which is associated with the end rather than the beginning or next phase in your career. But I believe that it is too late to only start thinking about legacy in the few years leading up to retirement. Instead, your legacy begins to come to life from the moment you step into the working world.

This view is based on Glen Llopis' definition of legacy: "that which represents your body of work at each stage of your career as you establish the foundational building blocks and accumulate the required wisdom to grow your passion".[17] This definition makes it clear that you leave a legacy at each stage of your career. Your legacy grows with each new experience you have, with each new idea you implement, and each time you inspire others to achieve something new. Legacy is the creation of good for others and for future generations.

I believe each one of us has an opportunity to build our legacy every day of our lives and of our careers. Just like you enjoy and benefit from reading about others who created, wrote or developed good books, tools or any resources that you find useful in your life, you also have an opportunity – and, in my opinion, a responsibility – to contribute to the knowledge and resources available to future generations. Creating a legacy happens as you interact with people in your area of passion and as you grow your career.

A legacy is therefore not a room named in your honour or an engraving on a plaque; it is something, whether tangible or intangible, that you did to add value to individuals you worked with or to the organisation you work for. A legacy captures your story, the things you did, places you went to, goals you accomplished, your failures, and more. It is something that you as a person leave behind to be remembered by.

Why is leaving a legacy important?

Legacies are important because they can become pathways that guide other people in decisions about what to do or not to do with their careers. As you share your past experiences with others, they get to learn from your successes and your mistakes, thereby helping them not to go through the same learning curves that you went through as you were building your career. If you are passionate about your career and what you do, you will want to leave a mark and create a legacy for people to benefit from.

Some iconic legacies have shaped entire industries.

Steve Jobs shaped the smartphones industry. And Kim Kardashian, for example, disrupted the entire entertainment industry and created success from reality television. Think about these two individuals. You might be intrigued that I even put these names together in one paragraph but they have something big in common: their careers and business were about their passions and they have both left an impressive legacy.

Leaving a legacy contributes to your own personal development. Knowing that what you do now will affect others in the future motivates you to constantly strive to do better and have a positive impact on everyone you encounter. You grow from the process. Furthermore, your legacy can contribute directly to the growth of your profession. You can offer new innovative ways of doing things. The entertainment industry will never be the same again after Kim Kardashian and her contribution through reality television. If you look at smartphones, can you even imagine what would they be without Steve Jobs having contributed his innovation and leadership in the development and growth of this industry? Whatever your industry, as you grow your passion and contribute new ways for creating impact, your profession also evolves.

Consider your legacy as something that you will always be remembered by. It is an output of your lifelong career. The amount of wealth you acquire throughout your career is useful but it cannot be equated to the legacy you leave. Your legacy is priceless. Once you have gone through your work life, you cannot go back and start again to leave a different legacy. You can look at it the same way as your personal brand; the only difference is that it is a reflection of your lifetime of work and achievements.

How do you create your legacy?

So how can you create a positive legacy at the same time as you enjoy your career and grow your passion?

1. Be clear on your principles and beliefs, communicate them in your work, and live by them. Some people even suggest creating a personal mission statement and basing your actions on this. It is those actions that people will remember you for when you are not there. Knowing what's important, what drives you and how you want to be remembered creates tremendous clarity in how you communicate your beliefs and principles. You can then clarify these at every opportunity day-to-day. Once you have defined these, it is important that you treat everyone in a manner that reflects your beliefs. For example, in my line of work, I believe that each person can learn to do a job they like, as long as they have a passion to do it and they have a positive attitude. The way I treat everyone is in line with this belief.

2. Be clear on the impact your job, your career is having on others, on the environment and the overall business. You create a positive legacy by impacting others positively.

3. Use every opportunity to share your skills and experience with others. This is about you sharing what you have learned as you've grown and developed in your career. There are a number of ways to do this; for example, you might coach others who are in the same job as you, or who are still growing to get to where you are. Or you might mentor others, providing guidance on how they can also grow their careers, learning from your own personal experiences. What do you wish someone had shared with you at the beginning of your career?

4. Innovate. Find new ways of doing things or creating new products to solve daily problems. This kind of legacy will influence the evolution of your profession and industry for decades to come.

Here, I reiterate my belief that we all have an opportunity to build and leave a legacy. It doesn't matter where your career journey takes you – you are leaving impressions every day, so it's worth making sure that those impressions are valuable. You start building your legacy the very first day you start working – you do not wait until it is time for your retirement to start thinking about what legacy you are creating in your career.

Self-reflection Questions

1. If I were to ask my colleagues about my legacy they will say …

2. Three characteristics that I want my career legacy to be are …

3. Action I'm willing to take to build this legacy is …

4. The impact I want to have on others is …

MONETISE YOUR PASSION

"What can others learn from you?"

What if you could share your expertise for a living? More and more people are realising that the greatest asset they have in this world is their knowledge, experience and the legacy they have built. As knowledge become more valuable a number of industries are emerging within the knowledge economy. This has led to a growing demand for experts in various fields.

The expert industry is about sharing your expertise and lessons you have learnt from your career. The industry is built on two principles. First, each of us is an expert at something, even if we might not think so. Second, our expertise is worth sharing and has real value to others. You may not think of yourself as an expert, but you have accumulated a wealth of expertise which others would value. The rise of the expert economy creates a marketplace for the knowledge, lessons, and wisdom you have gathered. This is echoed by an executive from Gerson Lehrman, one of the big pioneers of the expert industry, who maintains "Everyone is an expert at something, they just may not know it yet." A report by Bruce Reed and Matthew Atwell predicts that in 2018 the expert industry will become a billion-dollar business. What an opportunity![19]

In this chapter, I focus on how you can make a living sharing your knowledge and expertise by monetising what you've learnt throughout your career. What you know and who you are has value in the market place. You have learnt lessons in life that you can use to help other people get ahead faster. To illustrate this point, ask yourself: Have you seen an increase in the number of people that are offering help to others on various topics, such as starting your business, living your passion, and so on? Those individuals are like you and me. What they are doing is consolidating and packaging their knowledge and life experiences into chunks that can be offered to others for authentic personal improvement.

In his book *The Millionaire Messenger*, Brendon Buchard informs readers that their lives, knowledge and passion are far more important and have greater market value than they actually understand.[18] You are here to make a difference in this world and the best way to do that is to use your expertise, knowledge and experience to help others succeed.

Gregg Walker spent a decade as a Senior Vice President for Corporate Development at Sony Corporation of America. Before that, he was Vice President of Mergers and Acquisitions at Viacom and a Vice President at *Goldman Sachs*. In 2016 he started his own private investment firm. He has a law degree. Throughout his career he has earned various accolades including being named by *The Root*, [an Afrocentric online magazine that publishes an annual list of 100 most important black influencers] as the most powerful African American under 40. Walker now uses his expertise to advise clients looking to grow in the media and entertainment industry.

The key to entering the expert industry is to love helping others. You will succeed in this industry if you have a genuine passion for using your career experiences to help others create success. People like Brendon Buchard, Tony Robbins, and John Lee are the contemporary expert industry gurus; but there are many more who aren't regularly in the public eye but are making a big positive impact nonetheless.

Three ways of sharing your expertise

If you have used your career to build a track record that shows you managed to achieve results that others desire, your knowledge and experience become valuable; you can be what Brendon Buchard refers to as a *results expert*. You have been there, done that and can now help others.

On the other hand, if you are in touch with your passion, you may also delve into extensive research and study in a particular area, and become a research expert. As a *research expert* you are deeply knowledgeable about your field because you have researched it more than others have. What better way to learn more about your area of talent and make money at the same time?

Similarly, if you are someone who is easily trusted, admired and followed by others, you can also build your career as a *role model* expert. The world we live in has multiple platforms you can use to share what you know. There is an appetite for knowledge and new ideas, and people are willing to listen and engage you if you are able to highlight the value of your idea.

How can you monetise your career?

Monetising your career depends on your ability to package your knowledge and experiences in a way that is valuable to others. This also means creating a personal brand as an expert in your specific field.

You could start with the following suggestions:

1. *Packaged ready-to-go knowledge products*. These can include books, video teaching materials, or audio teaching materials. Start by writing notes about what you know in your area of work. It all starts with what you know and what you have experienced. Most of us tend to underestimate how much we know and how valuable it can be to others. Starting to believe in what you know and the value of your experience is the beginning of your ability to commercialise your knowledge.

2. *Coaching and mentoring services*. As an expert you can provide coaching and mentoring services to others. I provide one-on-one coaching specifically for those who would like to transition to new careers.

3. *Events*. You can host events to teach about your expert area. This can be in a form of a one-day event focusing on a specific topic that you have built expertise in. For example, John Lee runs one-day events in property entrepreneurship.

4. *Specific services*. You can provide a *"done for you"* service where you offer to do a specific task on behalf of others, such as a ghostwriting service or writing or editing CVs on behalf of your clients.

5. *Join talent-on-demand networks*. More and more companies are using this concept. This is more like a gig for people with expertise. Well-known companies that you can join to sell your expertise are Upwork and Fiverr. PricewaterhouseCoopers launched its platform called Talent Exchange, an online market place for highly skilled independent talent interested in working on consulting projects for and with PWC clients.

6. *Join the expert network firm.* These firms keep a list of professionals who are paid by industry leaders for their specialised information and research services. They pair their clients with experts in a timely manner under conditions both parties can trust. The biggest operator in this field is Gerson Lehrman Group (GLG) who has over 600 000 experts in their network. At the end of this book, I have provided you with a list of other firms operating in this industry that you can join.

Critical success factors for the expert industry

In order to be successful in the expert industry you need the following characteristics:

- You must believe that you can be of value to others and be able to package your knowledge and expertise in a way that demonstrates value to your customers.

- You must be able to understand what people need and package what you know in a way that addresses their needs. As John Lee always asserts, you must be able to "sell people what they want and provide them with what they need".

- Because the job is all about transferring your expertise to others, having storytelling skills is critical. Whether you are a researcher, a coach or providing expert advice to companies, you must be able to tell your story in a way that others can understand, learn from, and be able to make business or personal decisions from it.

- Personal branding is important for success in the expert industry. Clients want to know your track record and your accolades. They want to know what you have done in your own career, what you have personally achieved with your career. They also want a proven track record of how you have helped others in your specific field of work. Think about it, if you are going to hire me as your coach or mentor, you will want to know that you will receive value that will help you solve the problem you want to solve. This is why building your personal brand and your legacy as you build your career is important.

- Social Media and collaborative platforms are the primary channels for connecting with potential customers within the expert economy. Your presence on platforms like LinkedIn, Twitter, and Facebook is crucial to building your brand, sharing your expertise and in connecting with potential clients. In addition, expert network firms such as GLG use online platforms to connect you with potential clients.

We are learning more about the expert industry as it grows, and there are undoubtedly as yet undiscovered realms of success for creative and innovative experts to explore.

I conclude by reminding you that your career journey can be truly valuable to others. Reed and Atwell[19] observed that "the most profound aspect of the expert industry is the recognition that the lessons from your career and life are of genuine value to others". With this in mind, you can create a valuable product to sell to others. But you must carefully craft your career much earlier – as taught in all of the steps preceding this one – so that you can learn, grow and gain valuable experiences that will later become of value to others.

Self-reflection Questions

1. The value and knowledge I have built throughout my career that I can sell to others is …

2. I can package and deliver this value by creating the following products …

3. The reason I believe my offering will be helpful to others is …

Chapter 10

TEN PRINCIPLES OF MANAGING YOUR CAREER SUCCESSFULLY

In this chapter, I share ten basic principles that are crucial to observe if you are going to manage your career successfully. These I have observed myself and I have also witnessed them in others who have created success while following their passion.

1.   You own your career

This is the basic and most important of the principles. It speaks to ownership of who you want to be and what you want to do with your life. You are the driver of where your career goes. There will be people in your life who will have a significant influence on your life decisions and career choices – such as your parents, peers, your teachers, mentors and coaches you meet along the way. Learn from these people as much as you can. But remember that at the end of the day, the decision about your career is yours. You'll never be able to make everyone happy – there will always be people who disapprove of your choices. So focus on you: what makes you happy? And the rest will follow.

This becomes important in times when you have to make tough and at times selfish decisions. Sometimes your parents would like you to choose a particular career, and they try to steer you that way. Some people follow that guidance and find themselves unhappy in unfulfilling careers.

By basing your decisions on the desires of others, you become restrained by other people's values and expectations. To put this in real terms: Candice recalls how her fear of disappointing her parents drove her to continue with her training as a doctor when she knew that her passion was on computers and graphic designing. By the time she graduated medical school, she knew that if she continued with a career as a doctor she'd be miserable for the rest of her life. She had aspired to her parents' ambition, and not her own. Was their happiness worth her misery?

How many times have you worried about what others will think if you decide to take a job that challenges what is expected of you? Hermina Ibarra[16] maintains that owning your career means breaking free from our "ought selves" – the identities created by important people in our lives.

2. Listen to what the universe is telling you

Learning to listen to what the universe is telling you about your career will enhance your freedom and confidence. The universe talks to us in various ways. The most common and noticeable one is through events that take place in your life and have a direct or indirect impact on your career. These are normally unplanned events which force you to make a decision – for example, redundancy, bad performance reviews, or losing out on a promotion you've worked hard to achieve. Such events push you to take stock of where you are in your career, and reconsider if it is time for a change.

While going through such events can be hurtful and may feel like the end of the world at times, the important thing to do as you move through them is to ask yourself, what can I learn from this experience; and what is the universe telling me about where I should be taking my career?

When I took on one of my Director roles, it was a turning point in my career. I poured my whole existence into making the job a success – and my personal life was non-existent. I worked long hours and weekends for the whole year. I was setting up a new function and it was important for me that it would be successful. When it came to the end-of-year review, I was disappointed to receive a rating below 100%. That sparked one of the most drastic career decisions I've ever made.

I started thinking about my career and where I was going with it. I decided to create boundaries between work and personal life. I became conscious of the hours I invest in my work and my personal and family time. I also decided to focus on developing myself even more so that I could start working on projects that I like. From then onwards any work I would do after hours would be focused on personal development and growing my passion. Finally, I was able to start writing more – and that's why you're reading this book right now!

3.   Always pass on knowledge to others

As you grow in your career and learn new skills, find time to pass knowledge on to others. The most common benefit of sharing knowledge is: the more you teach others, the more you learn yourself. Find ways to mentor other upcoming young talent in the same field of work. As you teach others you also embed your knowledge and become an expert in the subject you are teaching. Simultaneously, you build a network of protégés to collaborate with. As we discussed in more detail earlier, mentoring is two-way learning – you will always deepen your knowledge when you offer your expertise to others.

4.   Don't be too attached to a job title

In today's world of work, the *job title* has become very important. So much so that we sometimes lose sight of the overall job content and place all the importance on the title. Yes, an attractive job title looks good on your CV. However, an attractive job title with limited work content that does not allow you to develop depth in your skill is not beneficial. For example, one might choose a Director job for the title, instead of a Manager job – when actually that particular managerial role offers a broader scope for skill growth. Clients often tell me they're looking for a job with a specific title, and I am keen to remind them that their desired title is fine *only* if it offers the opportunity to gain the experience and skills necessary to progress in their career.

5.   Do not stay in a culture that will dampen your passion

Let's face it, the culture you work in can make or break your career. It is important to be aware of the impact that the leadership, the people you work with, and the ways of working in your organisation have on your role and on your passion for the job in general. Do not allow anyone to dampen your passion. If the people you work with or your company's culture make you feel disillusioned, always explore other options to find out whether you're really falling out of love with your passion or whether it's simply being broken by the job you're doing. If it's the latter, it's definitely time to seek a new position!

6. You receive what you give

This principle applies across the universe: you get what you give. Similarly, in your career whatever you do to help others with their careers, you will receive back. Inversely if you have been an impediment to others' careers, you will receive that back too. This means you want to have a positive impact on others' careers all the time. Open doors for young upcoming talent and support the growth and development of others. This is part of creating your legacy!

7. Seek to balance depth and breadth

There is value in changing jobs and experiencing different companies and different industries. You learn best practice from different perspectives. However, this might come at a cost. Constantly changing jobs means you are forever in a process of learning how to operate in a new environment. Take, for instance, a person who changes jobs every two years. Let's say this person has five years' experience. This means out of this experience only three years is real work experience; the other two years is time spent learning about the new environment. It takes about six months to a year to settle into a new company and learn the correct ways of doing things. Constantly changing jobs might provide you with exposure to multiple companies and different ways of applying your trade but it might not provide you with the depth of experience you need to build your skills. When reviewing CVs, recruiters will favour a CV with fewer companies and longer tenure than one with several jobs held for short periods of time.

8. Know when it is time to go (when it's time to go, it's time to go!)

I've come across many people who know in their heart of hearts that it's time to move on, but who keep holding on to the job. We do this for a number of reasons – because of loyalty to those we work for, or fear of trying something different, or sheer stubbornness. It's easier to carry on with what you know than branch out to something new. It is good to stay where you are wanted; but it's detrimental to stay in a job when there are strong indicators that it's time to leave.

When your emotional connection to the company starts dwindling, don't ignore this potentially strong signal that it's time to go. You see, we connect with our jobs intellectually because we are engaged by the task we do. We also connect with our jobs emotionally. Have you ever heard someone say "my heart does not want to be here anymore!" That means that logically the person knows they still need the job for one reason or another but they have lost the passion, the interest and inspiration that made them enjoy the role earlier on.

Ignoring signs that it is time to leave can be detrimental to your career. Take for example Pedro, a very experienced Marketing Director. When he joined his company he was highly regarded. He had been brought in by the CEO, and the two had known each other for a long time. Throughout his work with this employer, his success was mainly because of his relationship with the CEO. As a result, he was always on special important projects. While this worked for him, he did not build good relationships with other colleagues and negative feedback about him as a leader permeated throughout the organisation. When the CEO left the company, Pedro was placed in a redundancy program. It was clear to me that his career within this company was over. He would not have any sponsors now that the CEO had left.

Pedro did not realise this, and he kept looking for other opportunities to remain within the company. He missed out on the redundancy package and six months after moving into a new role he was let go due to performance issues. Pedro had failed to realise at the right time that it was time to go.

9. You are only loyal to yourself

I have heard people talk about how loyal they are to their employer to the extent that they would pass up amazing opportunities for fear of disappointing others. Loyalty is a valuable trait, but it is important to remember that you are in a business relationship – so any decision you make must be in your best interests. Your employer also has to make decisions based on the best interests of the business, and if it comes down to it, a company will always choose progress and financial success over supporting and developing your career. Therefore, when making career decisions remember that the first loyalty is to yourself. Be guided by what works best for you.

10. You can always use your current job to jumpstart your move to the next job

Never underestimate your current job or project – even if it seems meaningless. You have an opportunity to use it to prepare yourself for your next move. I often hear people speak of how their current job isn't even worth including on their CV. What I tell them is that even if you are doing an unpaid volunteering job, all the work you are doing is valuable and you can frame it in a way that sells you well for the next job. It starts with understanding the job you are doing and ensuring that no matter how boring and unchallenging it is, you find ways of learning a skill that you will use in the future. If the job is too easy, find ways of making it challenging and creating opportunities for yourself within it – be proactive, and every job can teach you something.

Sergio took a job as an administrative assistant, but he knew he would soon get bored of repetitive activities. After three months in this job he was struggling to remain motivated. Sergio's mentor challenged him to think of ways he could do his daily tasks in a different way. Sergio took the challenge and designed an automated file tracking system that made it easy for employee files to be stored, tracked and retrieved quickly. This process was eventually adopted by the whole company. This helped Sergio land his next job as a trainee process auditor with his current employer.

Not only did this help Sergio land a new job, but he built a track record of innovation and productivity that he could confidently include and highlight as a key achievement in his CV.

Chapter 11

LIMITS TO CAREER SUCCESS AND HOW TO AVOID THEM

As you continue with your career journey, you will face challenges that can block your progress. You should be able to immediately identify these and overcome them.

One such obstacle is working in a role where your next career move is dependent on someone else moving – and that person *has no intention of going anywhere* with their career. If your next promotion is dependent on your boss leaving, that could be a serious blocker to your career moving forward. In a situation like that it is important that you broaden your scope and look for external opportunities. Waiting for others to make life-changing decisions is *not* a productive way to manage your career. Waste no time; and if you really do have to wait, use that period to acquire experiences that you'll need in future.

Nereen had ambitions to be a General Manager in her region. She had been with her company for seven years. Nereen's team leader, Blake, had been with the company for 20 years. He had tried every job he wanted to and was not looking for any career move. He'd decided that the only thing that would motivate him to move would be an opportunity to work in a different country – but he was not prepared to relocate his family. So, he was staying put, and he still had 10 years before retirement.

For Nereen, this was a serious obstacle as she did not want to leave the company but was also conscious that her next move would not be until Blake moved on – a decade in the future. Nereen took the decision to move from sales to finance, which helped her learn about all the analytics that would make her successful as a General Manager. After two years as a Finance Analyst, Nereen moved to Supply Chain and spent three years in a role as a Demand Planner, which helped her understand how to manage customer supply and demand. At this point, Blake decided to take early retirement and Nereen was promoted to the General Manager role that she had always aspired to.

Nereen believes if she had stayed in one department while waiting for this opportunity, she would have left the company. But moving to different functions helped her with the wait, and also allowed her to acquire critical skills which supported her aspiration to become a general manager.

Another common career blocker is the politics at your place of work. I have heard people confess they hate politics and some have even left their jobs because they are trying to evade internal political conflict. The fact is politics is everywhere. There is no way of evading it. The key to managing politics is to build networks of likeminded colleagues, and align yourself with sponsors who will have your interests at heart should issues arise.

You maintain the support of these sponsors and networks by, in turn, supporting their journeys and projects. Be sure to be open about your career ambitions with your key sponsors. They should know where you intend to take your career so that they can support you with your moves, and let you know when they hear of suitable opportunities for development. Having a sponsor does not mean towing lines, or pandering to one person over others. It means building relationships that will support your career and propel you in your preferred direction.

Another common obstacle arises when you come across an attractive job opportunity which requires you to *drop your salary or move a level down* in your job. In most instances you are presented with a job you know will provide you with the experience that is important for your career success, or one which will be personally and emotionally satisfying for you. Do you *not* take the job because you want to keep your pay and benefits? Or will you accept a pay and status drop? There is no formula for dealing with this common dilemma. It is a personal decision that you make after considering the broader impact that the downgrade will have on your life and your family situation.

Perhaps the most common blocker to career movement is *lack of qualifications* required for your next move. This can be frustrating, especially if you have worked hard and have all the experience necessary. In some instances, you have the qualification but you do not have experience and no one will even dare give you the opportunity to gain the required experience. What can you do?

Depending on where you are in your career, you can look at graduate and internship opportunities. The best way of acquiring experience is volunteering. You are less likely to be turned down if you are offering your services to gain experience. This might not be ideal because you don't earn while you learn, but it *is* generally quick and effective. A six-month voluntary internship will be worth a lot on your CV.

Sometimes your next career move *requires you to relocate* to a different branch, region or even a different country. In most companies, for example, it is a prerequisite that those in senior leadership positions have experience of working in a different country outside their home-country. Relocating can have a big impact on you and your family – and this could be transformative in a positive way, or it could create great struggle. When deciding whether to relocate to gain the necessary experience it is important that you consider the impact on your family. It is also important to selfishly look at the relocation opportunity being offered from the perspectives of financial benefit, personal development, and overall impact to your future career goals. By assessing all of these factors together you'll be able to make the best decision for yourself and your loved ones.

Chapter 12

FUTURE CAREER TRENDS AND HOW TO FUTURE-PROOF YOUR CAREER

Throughout this book, I've touched upon the crucial importance of constantly developing and honing your skills in order to sustain and develop your career. Developing and reinventing your career is important in light of changes in the workplace.

As the economy, technology and work landscape change, our work changes too. Some of our skills remain relevant while others become obsolete.

There was a time when MS-Dos was a highly sought-after skill, but having that in your CV today won't help you get a job. This is because technological changes have rendered this skill more or less useless.

Similarly, the more companies adopt new technologies, the more certain skills will become less relevant. For example, there is a strong belief that office jobs will change as more administrative and clerical tasks become automated due to technological advancements. We're seeing it already every day – with self-service checkouts at the supermarket, and automated ticket machines at train stations.

In this chapter, I will share with you some business trends which will determine the skills that are going to be in demand in future, and look at how you can prepare yourself for the impact of these identified trends on your career. The intention of this chapter is not to instil fear that your job might become irrelevant in future; rather, it is to provide you with information that you can use to help you decide what skills you need to add to your repertoire. We all need to accept that our current expertise could be outdated a few years down the line, so we must seek to acquire new, relevant skills. Our ability to up-skill, re-skill and hone existing capabilities will become more important in the future.

Trend #1 – The rise of the collaborative economy requires collaborative skills

The collaborative economy is sometimes called the sharing economy. It covers a number of sectors and is rapidly emerging across the world. It is a new way to offer and use products and services through online platforms. At the core of the collaborative economy are the technological platforms that connect consumers. According to a study by *PwC*, globally the collaborative economy will generate $335 billion by 2025.[20]

Here are a few of the growing sectors within the collaborative economy:

- *Peer-to-peer accommodation:* households sharing access to unused space in their home or renting out a holiday home to travellers such as Airbnb.

- *Peer-to-peer transportation:* individuals sharing a ride, car or parking space with others such as Lyft and Uber.

- *On-demand household services:* freelancer marketplaces enabling households to access on-demand support with household tasks such as food delivery and DIY such as Deliveroo, Taskrabbit.

- *On-demand professional services:* freelancer marketplaces enabling businesses to access on-demand support with skills such as administration, consultancy and accountancy such as Fiverr, Upwork, and Veploy.

- *Collaborative finance:* individuals and businesses who invest, lend and borrow directly between each other, such as crowd-funding and peer-to-peer lending

The growth in this economy has led to the increase in independent workers – those who take advantage of these platforms and offer their skills or lease their assets to others. A 2016 McKinsey report on independent work and the gig economy reported that between 20 to 30% of the working age population in the US and EU or up to 162 million individuals engage in independent work.[21] Working in the sharing economy is characterised by a high level of individual control and autonomy, with payment by task assignment or sales, and projects or contracts are usually short term.

What can you do to prepare yourself for the collaborative economy?

For you to benefit from these platforms you need to *have specific skillsets that you are willing to sell.* Having a degree or certification is no longer that important, but possessing skills that are relevant to the needs of the market will make you successful in the sharing economy. As Diane Mulcahy observes, "The gig economy is an economy of skill and skilled workers are the winners who take all." [22]

Continuously building and sustaining skill sets that you can sell to your employer but that you can also use to take advantage of the opportunities presented by the gig economy is the best preparation you can do. While degrees and certificates are still good to have, having a core skill that is in demand will help you win in the collaborative economy.

Graphic design, web design, creating killer PowerPoint presentations, writing and editing are all valuable skills to deploy in the collaborative economy. Whatever your area of expertise is, sharpening your skill to an extent that you can sell it and deliver a valuable service to someone else will place you at an advantage.

Five actions to prepare yourself for the sharing economy:

1. Focus on building and honing your skills and make them valuable to others.

2. Continuously look for ways you can create value you can sell to others.

3. Build a career as a developer of the platforms or maintaining the platform.

4. Be an entrepreneur and start your own sharing platform aligned with your passion.

5. Coach others to prepare them to enter the sharing economy in your area of expertise.

Trend #2: The rise of the digital economy will require each employee to have basic digital skills

Digitisation covers a wide range of different digital technologies (e.g. computers, mobile devices, internet and the 'Internet of Things', robotics and automation), which have wide-ranging implications and impact in the workplace.

The World Economic Forum's 2016 analysis of the 'Future of jobs' defines the digitisation of the economy as the development in genetics, artificial intelligence, robotics, nano-technology, 3D printing and biotechnology, to name just a few, which will lay a foundation for extensive transformations in the way we live and work.[23]

The digital economy is now permeating the world economy, including retail (e-commerce), transportation (automated vehicles), education (online courses and remote learning), health (electronic records and personalised medicine), and social interactions and personal relationships (social networks). The digital economy has grown at an average annual rate of 5.6 % in the past 11 years through 2016, compared with 1.5% growth in the economy as a whole, according to the US Commerce Department's Bureau of Economic Analysis.

Some of the key features brought into the world of work by the growth of the digital economy include geographical location becoming irrelevant; the key role played by online platforms; the importance of network effects; and the use of big data. This has also resulted in new jobs becoming prevalent to support this evolving world of work.

Emerging new jobs from the digital economy

- big data architects,

- internet engineers,

- networking specialists,

- hardware engineers,

- mobile app developers,

- data scientists,

- and digital marketing specialists.

Digitisation has not only created new jobs, it has also brought about transformation in existing jobs, by changing work practices, best practice conventions, job content and job requirements and, as a consequence, the skills needed to perform the job.

A report by the European commission shows that in Europe 98% of workplaces require managers and 90% professionals (e.g. engineers, doctors and nurses, teachers, accountants, software developers, lawyers and journalists), technicians, clerical workers or skilled agricultural workers to have at least basic digital skills. 80% of workplaces require basic digital skills for sales workers. Workplaces also often require basic digital skills for building workers (50% of workplaces) and plant machine operators (34%).[24]

Some of the skills that have been identified as important for one to be successful in the digital economy include:

Basic digital skills that are a pre-requisite in the digital economy:

- Ability to communicate via email, social media/collaborative platforms, Skype/video calls.
- Ability to create or edit digital documents.
- Ability to search and find information using online platforms while protecting personal information online.
- Ability to communicate through ICT using email.

What can you do to prepare yourself for the growing digital economy?

It is important that you keep up to date on how this trend is impacting your career field. Keep abreast of how the digital trend is impacting your specific job and company, and what *new* jobs are being created as a result of the digital trend. It is also useful to learn about the new digital trends within your field and contribute, if possible, new ideas on how these can improve productivity in your company. My advice on preparing for this trend is to embrace it rather than fight it. Change is coming, whether you like it or not!

Five questions to ask yourself to assess the potential impact of the digital economy on your career/skill set:

1. What part of my job can be automated?

2. What skills will I require to support the automated part of my job?

3. What digital tools exist to make my job more efficient?

4. Which industries are growing more in my field of work and which are reducing as a result of the growing digital trend?

5. How can I continue to grow my career within the new digital economy?

Your answers to these questions will help jumpstart you into action to safeguard your future career against digital impact.

Trend #3: Virtual teams become the norm

The evolution of technology and availability of different technological platforms and digitisation of work have made it possible for us to be able to work from anywhere. This has led to the proliferation of virtual teams in the work place. A virtual team shares a common business objective, but the individual team members may be separated by time zones, geographic distance or organisational boundaries. What links members of a virtual team with each other and their organisation is communication, technology and directive, as communicated by the business and the team leader.

In a 2016 survey by Culture Wizard[25] (an organisation dedicated to study culture around the world) 48% of respondents revealed that more than half of their teams included members from other nations. Furthermore recent estimates by Global Workplace Analytics claim that about 3.2% of the global workforce works from home at least half of the time. With the number of people who work from home having increased by 103% since 2005, there is no denying that virtual teams are growing exponentially in the workplace.[26]

While the ability to work from any location can provide great flexibility and the freedom to choose a lifestyle most suited to you and your family, it does come with some challenges that you need to be aware of. One of the main challenges with working virtually is not being part of a physical team. You might have virtual team members that you are in contact with on a regular basis, but sometimes meeting with a person face to face might solve issues much quicker and produce much better results.

The success of a virtual team is dependent on trust among its members. Generally, trust is important in the success of all teams, however, it is even more important for team members that do not see each other often, whose jobs are dependent on each other. Your ability to build and sustain trust with colleagues around the world will become even more critical.

Another skill that will be in demand is the ability to work with people from diverse cultural backgrounds and being able to understand how different cultures operate. Leading a global team of professionals from across different cultural backgrounds was an eye opener for me. It took me a while to realise that leading someone from Russia had to be different from leading someone from Israel or the United Kingdom. Understanding individuals within their own cultural context is a skill that will make you successful in your virtual teams, hence the importance of taking overseas jobs as they are the best and easiest way to experience the world and learn about different cultures. Here are some additional skills required to be effective in working with virtual teams:

Five steps to prepare yourself to work effectively in a virtual team:

1. Learn to agree on a common team goal, no matter where you are based. If you have a common goal you are working towards, that makes you a team.

2. Learn to clarify team roles – even though you work from different locations if all of you are clear on what each one's contribution and role in the team is, you are more likely to be successful as a team.

3. Learn to use collaborative tools to facilitate team collaboration; these include video conferencing tools.

4. Learn about the different cultures of your colleagues based in different countries.

5. Learn different techniques to communicate with colleagues based in different locations.

Trend #4: Artificial intelligence and robotics at work

Artificial intelligence and robots are often spoken about as a potentially dangerous phenomenon. I believe that they are simply tools created for the benefit of us humans. Consider Edward Bellamy's classic *Looking Backward*, in which the character Julian West wakes up from a 113-year slumber and finds the United States in year 2000 has changed dramatically from what it was in 1887. People stop working at age forty-five and devote their lives to mentoring other people and engaging in volunteer work that benefits the overall community. There are short work weeks for employees, and everyone receives full benefits, food, and housing.

The reason is that new technologies of the period in Bellamy's story – robots – have enabled people to be very productive while working part-time. Businesses do not need large numbers of employees, so individuals can devote most of their waking hours to hobbies, volunteering, and community service.

In conjunction with periodic work stints, they have time to pursue new skills and personal identities that are independent of their job.

Such a world might sound like a farfetched dream. But an analysis of 750 jobs by the *McKinsey Global Institute* concluded that 45% of paid activities could be automated using technologies that are already in functional use, and 60% of occupations existing today could have 30% or more of their processes automated.[27] Another McKinsey report, *"Jobs Lost, Jobs Gained"*, found that 30% of current work activities could be automated by 2030 and 375 million workers worldwide could be affected by emerging technologies.[28]

In an interview with *The Economist*,[29] Google Vice President [Vint Cerf] reminds us that "on the whole, robots and intelligent software seem destined to be used in cooperative and collaborative ways with humans." The common emerging understanding of how humans will work with robotics is that it will augment human capacity with machine intelligence. For example, the breakdown and analysis of large quantities of information and pattern recognition are some of the ways in which robotic systems and software can be used to assist human endeavour. Manufacturers such as Airbus and Nissan are already finding ways to use collaborative robots, or "co-bots", which work side by side with workers in factories.

While I don't want you to enter a state of panic about the arrival of robots and artificial intelligence in our places of work, it is important to realise that employers are currently working on implementing automation in areas where it is deemed to be economically efficient to do so. A study conducted by Deloitte in 2018 found that 61% of organisations were actively redesigning jobs around artificial intelligence (AI), robotics, and new business models, and 42% believed automation would have a major impact on job roles over the next two years. [14] This disruptive change has huge implications for workforce needs, including skills that will be in demand.

It will result in scrapping the traditional "up or out" career ladder in favour of careers where people can continuously re-skill, gain new experiences, and reinvent themselves at work

While some people believe there will be job losses as a result of the introduction of robots in the workplace, research suggests that robots will improve scale, speed, and quality, but not necessarily do away with jobs. In fact, it might do just the opposite.

This is in line with Boston University professor James Bessen's research findings that occupations with higher levels of computerisation and technology experience higher rates of employment growth. However for this to happen, the new technology must be improving productivity in markets that have large unmet needs.[30]

What's more, in many cases, the newly created jobs are more service-oriented, interpretive, and social. For example, an increase in roles that are based on the *increased use of technology* such as data analysts scientists, application and software developers, ecommerce and social media specialists.

It is further projected that *roles that leverage human skills* are also on the increase such as customer service workers, sales and marketing roles, training and development roles, people and culture roles, as well as innovation managers.

The trend is clear – an increase in innovative technology development skills and human-related skills while the decrease is in manual activity-driven skills as demonstrated in Table 1.3 below.

Table 1.3 Comparing top 10 skills in demand and declining

Increasing demand 2018	Increasing demand 2022	Declining in demand 2022
Analytical thinking and innovation	Analytical thinking and innovation	Manual dexterity, endurance and precision
Complex problem-solving	Active learning and learning strategies	Memory, verbal, auditory and spatial abilities
Critical thinking and analysis	Creativity, originality and initiative	Management of financial, material resources
Active learning and learning strategies	Technology design and programming	Technology installation and maintenance
Creativity, originality and initiative	Critical thinking and analysis	Reading, writing, math and active listening
Attention to detail, trustworthiness Emotional intelligence	Complex problem-solving	Management of personnel
Reasoning, problem-solving and ideation	Leadership and social influence	Quality control and safety awareness
Leadership and social influence	Emotional intelligence Reasoning, problem-solving and ideation	Coordination and time management
Coordination and time management	Systems analysis and evaluation	Visual, auditory and speech abilities
		Technology use, monitoring and control

Source: Future of jobs survey 2018, World Economic Forum

Four steps you can take to prepare yourself for the robotics era:

1. Explore how your job is impacted by Artificial Intelligence. You can use this site to check the likelihood of your job being impacted: https://www. bbc.co.uk/news/technology-34066941

2. Focus on learning human skillsets such as emotional intelligence and skills that differentiate human workers from AI such as creativity, adaptability, and interpersonal skills.

3. Excelling in creative problem-solving, redefining problems and opportunities, coming up with new approaches, and taking action are key characteristics of creative problem-solving

4. Become curious and flexible. Curiosity and flexibility have always been important, but in the age of AI they are exponentially more critical.

5. Learn computer programming or coding skills – machine learning will rely on computer programmers.

Trend #5: The rise of blockchain and cryptocurrencies

A discussion about cryptocurrencies and blockchain often sounds complicated, and as a result it is easy to push aside and choose to ignore it. My advice is to not ignore this trend – it is one that will bring a major revolution in the world of work and eventually impact our careers.

So, what is it? Blockchain started as Bitcoin's 'operating system', recording financial transactions between two people, and thereby cutting out the middleman (the bank). It has the ability to record almost anything on a digitally distributed database. It is, effectively, a database which is peer-validated by a wider community, rather than a central authority.[31]

It is already predicted that in the near future, all documents will be on the blockchain: passports, ID-cards, medical records, letters of credit, freight & customs documents, hotel & flight bookings, and so on and so forth. There will be no more errors, and no possibility for corruption. Society will become a blockchain-based purpose-economy, where you can subscribe to global peer-to-peer networks to find jobs you like doing, which will pay you in cryptocurrency by the minute.[32] If all the jargon bores you, all you need to remember about blockchain is that just as e-mail enabled bilateral messaging, blockchain enables bilateral financial transactions. This will definitely impact the world of work *and* our careers.

As of November 2017, there were over 1,324 different cryptocurrencies in circulation, and they are growing fast.

There will come a point when we will all have to understand how the world of cryptocurrency works as more and more businesses start accepting cryptocurrencies as form of payment. I foresee a day in future where we can choose whether we get paid in hard currency or cryptocurrency – imagine that!

How the blockchain revolution evolves will impact existing jobs. How we do our work now will change; we will have to learn and develop new skills to remain in these jobs.

The way we find jobs will also change. If you look at companies like Jobcoin, you will see how they are using jobcoins (cryptocurrency) to pay workers. Employers can advertise jobs internationally and pay employees using the global jobcoins. You can interact with and get hired by employers using their freelance platform, Jobstoday. Once you have completed the job, you are then paid through their global jobscoin.[33]

Five actions to take to prepare your career for blockchain and cryptocurrencies:

1. Read about blockchain cryptocurrencies – don't let the technical jargon turn you off.

2. Consider getting into a career in blockchain, it's new and everyone is learning – what a great time to start a new career.

3. Figure out a way that you can contribute to this field with the talents you already have.

4. Software development will be crucial for the success of the cryptocurrency industry – you could choose to build a career in this field.

5. Map out industries where blockchain technology makes the most sense. These include the insurance industry, banking and supply chain management. Find out what their future plans are and how you can prepare yourself to be part of those.

Trend #6: The individual and their career takes centre stage

With the growth of individualised and personalised services across all spectrums of business, careers will also become more individualised. Instead of a steady career progression along a job-based pathway, organisations are forced to shift towards a model that empowers individuals to acquire valuable experiences, explore new roles, and continually reinvent themselves.

Careers are no longer narrowly defined by jobs and skills but through experiences and learning agility. The ongoing transformation of work brought about by the technology revolution we are experiencing, the need for people and organisations to constantly upgrade capabilities, and changes in employee preferences will lead to new approaches to how learning happens, how jobs are designed, how performance is managed, and how our careers develop.

Deloitte calls this "the 21st-century career". Careers are now made up of a series of developmental experiences, each offering you an opportunity to acquire new skills, perspectives, and judgement. Instead of following upward progress, careers in this century now follow an upward arc, with progression and promotion at various times, but they will look nothing like the simple stair-step path of generations ago. Today only 19% of companies still have traditional functional career models.[34]

What can you do to prepare yourself for the 21st century career?

Agility and willingness to learn new skills has become more important than ever for you. As technology changes, skills are becoming obsolete at a rapid rate. Do not expect a well laid out career ladder that you can climb. In fact, you don't want that – it's too limiting. Once you start climbing one ladder you are stuck with it and it becomes difficult to do something different.

The 21st century career approach allows you to perpetually acquire new skills, grow yourself and move along to related jobs and projects. It gives you ownership of your career, while the employer just provides learning resources for you to use in enriching your career. The challenge is to know how to manage your career and use all these available resources.

Five actions to take to prepare yourself for the 21st century career:

1. Identify experiences you require.
2. Identify roles or jobs that will help you to acquire these experiences.
3. Know which of your skills are becoming obsolete and which new skills you will be learning.
4. Discuss and align on your plan with your team leader.
5. Change jobs, employers or industries to acquire new skills and experiences.

As organisations are moving towards flatter structures, there are fewer management opportunities and less focus on upward career progression. I started out as a junior HR consultant, progressed to a senior HR consultant, and then a junior manager – up till I reached the Director level. Career ladders like this are diminishing. You need to be ready for a more dynamic way of managing your career, focused on you and driven by you.

Are you ready?

Conclusion

The intention of this book is to provide you with actionable steps for identifying your passion and translating it into a successful career. If you commit to the nine steps and take action based on the advice laid out in these pages, you will dramatically accelerate your career. You will grow, flourish, and achieve professional satisfaction.

It does not matter where you are with your career right now. You have the freedom to redirect towards having a career that you are passionate about.

I have provided you with a guide for identifying your talents and areas of passion – and these are the key elements that drive your career success. I have highlighted the importance of building relevant skills and knowledge around your talents so that you can be ready to take advantage of available career opportunities. The role of a mentor in preparing and supporting you as you build a career from your passion has also been explored.

With this understanding you are able to sift through career choices in order to find your ideal job. You can settle upon the industry that you believe will be best suited to your passion and the relevant geography where you think your career will thrive. We have also looked at how to prepare for interviews. I have provided you with tools you can use to prepare yourself to be interviewed, and key questions you need to ask to determine if a job will be suited to your talent and passion.

The importance of growing your career and building your legacy throughout the different jobs you do along the way, and how you interact with others as you go on with your career, have also been discussed. I have highlighted the importance of clarifying what it is that you want to be known for and living your career the way you want to be known.

We all have our special talents and vocation. Your passion is stirred up when you work on activities that are aligned with your talents and strengths. The more you work in the field closely aligned to your passion the more you enjoy your work and thrive. This is why it is important that when looking for a job, you do not only look at whether you meet the job requirements, but also focus on whether the job ignites the spark of passion within you. You will be more successful if you focus on developing yourself around activities that you are passionate about!

If you've been working for a while and have changed jobs a number of times, you might have already used some of the approaches I have described in this book. You will relate to some of the methods and situations discussed; but some of the beliefs you hold surrounding the world of work, and the angle from which you seek new professional roles, will be reshaped as you work through the nine steps.

If you find you have grown in a career that you are not passionate about, you have the option to reinvent yourself and transition into something you like. Really – you can do this. And when you do, you'll experience an empowering sense of liberation. I have shared with you some key lessons from those who have successfully transitioned into careers they love with the hope that this will serve as your stepping stone into a career fuelled by your passion.

Whether you're right at the start of your career, or somewhere in the middle, feeling the pull of new opportunities, prepare yourself – now – for change.

Prepare to discover the power of your passion. Ready yourself for a transitional time and accept that it won't always be easy. But trust that it will be worth it.

Finally, should you wish to get in touch for clarifications of any topics covered in the book and for coaching, you can contact me at gugu.khazi@ passiontocareers.com

Useful Resources

Identifying your passion

https://thepassiontest.com passion profile quiz

http://www.self-directed-search.com

Identifying your strengths

https:// http://www.viacharacter.org/www/ https://totalsdi.com/
assessments/

put-your-brand-on-a-personalized-report/ https://www.savilleassessment.
com/work-strengths https://www.mbtionline.com/?utm_
source=MBF&utm_medium=link& utm_campaign=online

Choosing your career

https://www.how2become.com/ https://www.prospects.ac.uk/planner
https://targetjobs.co.uk/careers-advice/career-planning

Job search

Below is a list of career search engines that have jobs listed in different countries. https://www.jibberjobber.com/login.php

Monster International JobsMonster International Jobs
https://www.monster.com/geo/siteselection

CareerJet
http://careersjet.blogspot.com/2010/11/jobs-in-worldwide. html

CareerBuilder International
https://www.careerbuilder.com/jobseeker/jobs/jobfindil.aspx

Preparing your CV

https://www.totaljobs.com/careers-advice/ cvs-and-applications/which-cv
https://www.myperfectcv.co.uk https://intranet.birmingham.ac.uk/as/
employability/ careers/apply/cv/index. aspx

https://www.barclayslifeskills.com/i-want-help-applying-for-jobs/school/
cv-builder/

https://www.topcv.co.uk https://resunate.com http://resumup.com/choose
your_template

Preparing for interviews

https://www.barclayslifeskills.com/i-want-to-prepare-for-an-interview/
school/virtual-interview/
https://www.myinterviewpractice.com
https://biginterview.com

Determining suitable pay

https://www.payscale.com/index/UK

Find out about the culture of a prospective employer

https://www.glassdoor.co.uk/index. htm?countryRedirect=true

Preparing to start your new job

http://heatherhollick.com/files/First_90_Days_Worksheet- Leader.pdf

Developing & growing your career

https://www.eatyourcareer.com/2013/07/the-most-important-tool-for-
accelerating-your-career-growth/

Transitioning/changing careers

https://www.jobs.ac.uk/careers-advice/resources/ ebooks-and-toolkits/
career-change-toolkit National Careers Services
https://nationalcareersservice.direct.gov.uk/home

UK Course finder https://www.ukcoursefinder.com

Windmills http://www.windmillsonline.co.uk

Expert economy firms

Gerson Lehrman Group-https://glg.it

AlphaSights –
www.alphasights.com

Third Bridge www.thirdbridge.com

Guidepoint www.guidepoint.com

TAKE MASSIVE ACTION

WEEKLY PLANNER TO BE USED IN CONJUNCTION WITH PASSION TO CAREERS NINE-STEP MODEL

Please use the following weekly planner to make progress with the nine-step plan. The first plan is a suggested plan and the second one is a blank one for you to complete based on your own needs.

MONDAY	TUESDAY	WEDNESDAY	THURSDAY	FRIDAY
Discover your passion – use the passion quiz assessment to identify your main passion.	Identify a preferred culture for your passion – complete the OCAI culture assessment on pages 131 to 134 of the toolkit.	Create a Career Master-Plan – use the career planning template on pages 138 to 139 of the toolkit.	What career choices do you need to make right now? Answer the questions in step four considering where your career is right now.	Plan the legacy you want to leave in your career. Answer questions in step eight – what do you want to be known for in your whole career journey?
Complete the RIASEC assessment and identify your top three career interests.		Review step three – find a mentor. If you do not have a mentor explore potential mentors.		Plan to monetise your passion. Answer questions in step nine – what skills and knowledge are you building that you can monetise?

WEEKLY PLANNER TO BE USED IN CONJUNCTION WITH PASSION TO CAREERS

Complete the following blank planner based on your own needs and schedule.

MONDAY	TUESDAY	WEDNESDAY	THURSDAY	FRIDAY

Career Jumpstart Toolkit

This toolkit is suitable for those who are starting out in the world of work and looking for guidance on what careers to follow. It will also be useful to those that have been working for a while and are looking at ways to rejuvenate their careers.

The premise for this toolkit is based on a formula for career success that I have developed, which says: career success is achieved through combining passion, strengths and taking massive action.

> # Career Success =
> # Passion + Strengths x Action

Below is an explanation of each of the components of the formula. In this toolkit, I also recommend resources and tools that you can use in each component of the formula. Some of these resources are freely available online, while others have a fee attached. I have ensured that in each section you have a range of resources to choose from, with relevant links.

1. KNOW YOUR PASSIONS

Passion is one of our biggest gifts. Every one of us has individual gifts and strengths. If we can tap into these, then we can live successful and abundant lives. But in order for us to achieve this, we need to know and understand our passion.

a. Free Passion assessment

This quick seven-question test can reveal exactly how to discover your passions and create a life that you love! You can use this test to check if what you do is aligned with your passion and to discover what your passion is.

b. Passion quiz

This quiz gauges the ideal relationship between your career and your passion in life. In other words, it tells you how best to tie what you do for a living to something you are passionate about so that your career and life feel fulfilling, energising, and inspiring to you.

There are four possible outcomes: You can either be a **Firestarter, Tribe Member, Side Hustler, or Thriver**. Think of these four Passion Profiles like the four points on a compass. Knowing which major direction suits you will allow you to walk the right path. And once you're on the right path, it's so much easier to figure out the finer details of your passion.

2. KNOW YOUR STRENGTHS

A strength is the ability to consistently provide near-perfect performance in a specific activity. The key to building a strength is to identify your dominant talents, then complement them by acquiring knowledge and skills pertinent to the activity. Below are some useful strength assessment tools:

a. Gallup StrengthFinder

This assessment measures your natural talents within 34 themes and provides a life-changing lens for self-awareness. It also assists you with a language to more accurately describe what you do best. You will also have action items and in-depth information to use as you set out to accomplish your goals.

b. High5 Strength Test

This is a free strengths test that helps you know what you are really good at. The goal of this test is to educate people to do what they are normally good at. It aims to help professionals make happier conscious career choices by focusing and building upon what they are naturally good at.

c. The RichardStep Strengths and Weaknesses Aptitude test

This is a free test, recommended if any the following apply to you:

- You are looking for your strengths and weaknesses.
- You are looking for self-awareness, self-help, or life direction.
- You are looking for career or job ideas and direction.
- You are just curious or having some fun.

No matter your reason, by taking the test you are on your way to finding out some very interesting things about yourself and how you work inside. We spend so much time thinking about things happening on the outside – it's time to figure out what's happening on a deeper level.

3. CONNECT YOUR STRENGTHS TO CAREERS

You can use the Interest Profiler self-assessment (RIASEC) tool to help you identify what your interests are and translate them into occupations that best fit your profile.

In the following pages you'll find 60 questions regarding common work activities. By answering questions that represent important Interest Areas, the results from the Interest Profiler will help you discover your strong work-related interests and match them to potential careers.

Instructions for taking the RIASEC test

- Read the work activities from top to bottom and answer in the correct order.
- Read each question carefully and decide how you would feel about doing each type of work. Try not to think about whether you have enough education or training to do the work, or how much money you would make doing the work. Just think about whether you would like or dislike performing the work activity.
- **If you agree with the statement fill in the circle.** If you don't agree, leave the circle blank. There are no wrong answers.

❶ Take the RIASEC test

	1	2	3	4	5	6
1. I like to work on cars	O					
2. I like to do puzzles		O				
3. I am good at working independently			O			
4. I like to work in teams				O		
5. I am an ambitious person, I set goals for myself					O	
6. I like to organise things, (files, desks/offices)						O
7. I like to build things	O					
8. I like to read about art and music		O				
9. I like to have clear instructions to follow						O
10. I like to try to influence or persuade people					O	
11. I like to do experiments		O				
12. I like to teach or train people				O		
13. I like trying to help people solve their problems				O		
14. I like to take care of animals	O					
15. I wouldn't mind working eight hours per day in an office						O
16. I like selling things					O	
17. I enjoy creative writing			O			

18. I enjoy science		O				
19. I am quick to take on new responsibilities					O	
20. I am interested in healing people				O		
21. I enjoy trying to figure out how things work		O				
22. I like putting things together or assembling things	O					
23. I am a creative person			O			
24. I pay attention to details						O
25. I like to do filing or typing						O
26. I like to analyse things (problems/ situations)		O				
27. I like to play instruments or sing			O			
28. I enjoy learning about other cultures				O		
29. I would like to start my own business					O	
30. I like to cook	O					
31. I like acting in plays			O			
32. I am a practical person	O					
33. I like working with numbers or charts		O				

	R	I	A	S	E	C
34. I like to get into discussions about issues				O		
35. I am good at keeping records of my work						O
36. I like to lead					O	
37. I like working outdoors	O					
38. I would like to work in an office						O
39. I'm good at math I'm good at math		O				
40. I like helping people		O				
41. I like to draw			O			
42. I like to give speeches					O	
Grand Total						
	R	I	A	S	E	C

HALLAND, J. MAKING VOCATIONAL CHOICES: THEORY OF CAREERS. 1st Ed., ©1973. Reprinted by permission of Pearson Education, Inc, New York

❷ Add up the number of filled circles in each column and write the total for each column on the row labelled "grand total".

Using your grand total scores from above, transfer the scores for each letter into the appropriate column below.

R = Realistic Total:
I = Investigative Total:
A = Artistic Total:
S = Social Total:
E = Enterprising Total:
C = Conventional Total:

❸ Take the three letters with the highest scores and record them under "My Interest Code".

Have a look at what each career cluster means!

Realistic – The "Doers": People with Realistic interests like work activities that include practical, hands-on problems and solutions. They enjoy dealing with plants, animals, and real-world materials like wood, tools, and machinery. They often enjoy outside work. Often people with Realistic interests do not like occupations that mainly involve doing paperwork or working closely with others. Famous realists: TV carpenter Norm Abram, snowboarder Chloe Kim, and celebrity mechanic Jesse James.

Investigative – The "Thinkers": People with Investigative interests like work activities that have to do with ideas and thinking more than with physical activity. They prefer to search for facts and figure out problems mentally rather than to persuade or lead people. Prominent investigators: astrophysicist Neil deGrasse Tyson, primatologist Jane Goodall, mathematician/ computer scientist Grace Murray Hopper, and theoretical physicist Steven Hawking.

Artistic – The Creators: People with artistic interests like work activities that deal with the artistic side of things, such as forms, designs, and patterns. They like self-expression in their work. They prefer settings where work can be done without following a clear set of rules. Well-known artists include: painter/sculptor Leonardo da Vinci, actress Halle Berry, writer J.K Rowling and singer Beyoncé.

Social – The Helpers: People with social interests like work activities that assist others and promote learning and personal development. They prefer to communicate more than work with objects, machines or data. They like to teach, give advice or be of service to others. Famous helpers: Oprah, Dr Martin Luther King, TV psychologist Dr Phil McGraw.

Enterprising – The Persuaders: People with enterprising interests like work activities that have to do with starting up and carrying out projects, especially business ventures. They like persuading and leading people and making decisions. They enjoy taking risks for profit. These people prefer action rather than thought. Prominent persuaders include business magnate Jeff Bezos, entrepreneur Elon Musk.

Conventional – The Organisers: People with conventional interests who follow procedures and maintain accurate written and numerical business records. They prefer working in structured settings where roles and tasks are clearly defined. Well-known organisers are lawyers, financial managers, analysts.

❹ Check career pathways aligned to your interests

With your interest code and the different career clusters in hand, you can look at occupations that match your interests and career pathways. Identify the career pathway that is related to your top two interests identified in the RIASEC assessment.

R = Realistic

These people are often good at mechanical or athletic jobs. Good college majors for realistic people are:

	Related pathways
• Agriculture	Natural resources
• Health Assistant	Health services
• Computers	
• Construction	Industrial and engineering
• Mechanic/mechanist	technology
• Engineering	
• Food and Hospitality	Art and communication

I = Investigative

These people like to watch, learn, analyse and solve problems. Good college majors for investigative people are:

	Related pathways
• Marine biologist	Health services
• Engineering	
• Chemistry	Business
• Zoology	
• Medicine/Surgery	Public and human services
• Consumer economics	Industrial and engineering
• Psychology	technology

A = Artistic

These people like to work in unstructured situations where they can use their creativity. Good majors for artistic people are:

	Related pathways
• Communications	Public and human services
• Cosmetology	
• Fine and performing arts	
• Photography	Arts & communication
• Radio and TV	
• Interior Design	
• Architecture	

S = Social

These people like to work with other people rather than things. Good college majors for social people are:

	Related pathways
• Counselling	Public and human services
• Nursing	
• Physical therapy	
• Travel	Arts & communication
• Advertising	
• Public relations	
• Education	

E = Enterprising

These people like to work with others and enjoy persuading and performing. Good college majors for enterprising people are:

	Related pathways
• Fashion and Merchandising	Business
• Real estate	Public & human services
• Marketing/Sales	
• Law	Arts & communication
• Political Science	
• International Trade	
• Banking/Finance	

C = Conventional

These people are very detail oriented, organised and like to work with data. Good college majors for conventional people are:

	Related pathways
• Accounting	Health services
• Court reporting	
• Insurance	Business
• Administration	
• Medical Records	Industrial and engineering technology
• Banking	
• Data processing	

Source: O*NET Online onetonline.org/find/career

4. What is your preferred company culture?

Instructions: Using the OCAI (Organisational Culture Assessment Instrument) questionnaire, rate your current and preferred company culture using the statements below. If you are currently not working, focus on your preferred culture. For the current culture, you have 100 points to split across the statements according to your observed culture. For the preferred culture column allocate points to the statement that best describes the organisation you prefer. For each column the subtotal must add back to 100 points.

		CURRENT		PREFERRED
I	**Dominant characteristics**			
A	The organisation is a very personal place. It is a lot like an extended family people seem to share a lot of themselves			
B	The organisation is very dynamic and entrepreneurial. People are willing to stick their necks out and take risks			
C	The organisation is very results oriented. A major concern is with getting the job done. People are very competitive and achievement oriented			
D	The organisation is a very controlled and structured place. Formal procedures generally govern what people do			
	Subtotal			
	Enter values on the grey cell above until the subtotal is 100			

		CURRENT		PREFERRED
II	**Organisational Leadership**			
A	The leadership in the organisation is generally considered to exemplify mentoring, facilitating, or nurturing			
B	The leadership in the organisation is generally considered to exemplify entrepreneurship, innovation and risk			
C	The leadership in the organisation is generally considered to exemplify a no nonsense, aggressive, results-oriented focus			
D	The leadership in the organisation is generally considered to exemplify coordination, organising, or smooth-running efficiency			
	Subtotal			
	Enter values on the grey cell above until the subtotal is 100			

III	Management of employees			
A	The management style in the organisation is characterised by teamwork, consensus and participation			
B	The management style in the organisation is characterised by individual risk-taking, innovation, freedom and uniqueness			
C	The management style in the organisation is characterised by hard- driving competitiveness, high demands and achievement			
D	The management style in the organisation is characterised by security of employment, conformity, predictability and stability in relationships			
	Subtotal			
	Enter values on the grey cell above until the subtotal is 100			

IV	Organisational glue			
A	The glue that holds the organisation together is loyalty, mutual trust. Commitment to this organisation runs high			
B	The glue that holds the organisation together is commitment to innovation and development. There is an emphasis on being on the cutting edge			
C	The glue that holds the organisation together is achievement and goal accomplishment. Aggressiveness and winning are common themes			
D	The glue that holds the organisation together is formal rules and policies. Maintaining a smooth- running organisation is important			
	Subtotal			
	Enter values on the grey cell above until the subtotal is 100			

V	Strategic emphases			
A	The organisation emphasises human development, high trust, openness and participation persist			
B	The organisation emphasises acquiring new resources and creating new challenges. Trying new things and prospecting for opportunities are valued			
C	The organisation emphasises competitive actions and achievement. Hitting stretch targets and winning in the market place are dominant			
D	The organisation emphasises permanence and stability. Efficiency, control and smooth operations are important			
	Subtotal			
	Enter values on the grey cell above until the subtotal is 100			

VI	Criteria for success			
A	The organisation defines success on the basis of the development of human resources, teamwork, employee commitment and concern for people			
B	The organisation defines success on having the most unique or newest products. It is a product leader and innovator			
C	The organisation defines success on the basis of winning in the market and outpacing the competition. Competitive market leadership is key			
D	The organisation defines success on the basis of efficiency. Dependable delivery, smooth scheduling and low-cost production is critical			
	Subtotal			
	Enter values on the grey cell above until the subtotal is 100			

Organisational Culture Assessment Instrument (OCAI) reprinted with permission from the Quinn Association.

What company culture is right for you?

Now add all the answers to the different letters and show the tally below.

Totals		
Category	Current	Preferred
A		
B		
C		
D		

Using your scores above, plot your responses on the grid below to see your preferred culture. A high aggregate score on the A category means you are more comfortable working in the Clan culture. A high aggregate score for the B category means you are more comfortable working in the Adhocracy culture. Similarly, a high aggregate score on the C category means that you are more likely to be successful in the Market culture and lastly a high aggregate score on the D category means that you are more likely to be successful in the Hierarchical culture. The description and explanation of each of the cultures is provided on page 49. Remember there is no right or wrong culture – it is all about what is right for the organisation and if that works for you personally.

Flexibility & discretion

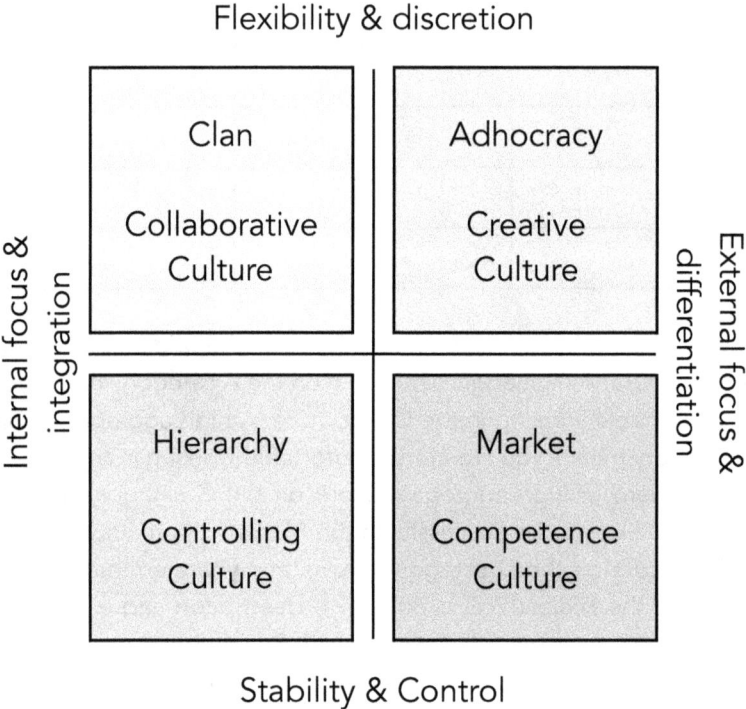

5. Take action

These are critical actions you need to focus on to build/revive or reinvent your career. Simply put, these actions will determine whether you accelerate your career, or you stagnate:

- Map out where you want to take your career (see career master plan).

- Identify your mentor (see criteria to identifying a suitable mentor).

- Make yourself visible in the market (see guidelines to make your CV & LinkedIn profile marketable).

- Prepare for interviews (see guide on how to prepare for interviews).

- Prepare for your first 90 days of success (see guideline for your first 90 days in your new job).

5.1 Create your career master plan

Use this form to think about your short-term and long-term career goals. What legacy do you want to leave for future generations and why that is important to you? **Start with Section D!**

Section A: Personal Mission Statement

In a broad statement describe what you strive to achieve with your career. For example:
"My mission is to give, for giving is what I do best and I can learn to do better. I will seek to learn, for learning is the basis for growth, and growing is the key to living. I will seek first to understand, for understanding is the key to finding value, and value is the basis for respect, decisions, and action. This should be my first act with my wife, my family, and my business. I want to help influence the future development of people and organisations. I want to teach my children and others to love and laugh, to learn and grow beyond their current bounds. I will build personal, business, and civic relationships by giving, in frequent little ways.
Mission statement:

Section B: Short-term career goals (1-3 years)	
What area of interest/position title would you like to see yourself working in?	What competencies/skills/ knowledge do you need to acquire: (areas I need to develop) to prepare for this move?

Section C: Long-term career goal (3-5 years)	
What area of interest/position title would you like to see yourself working in?	What competencies/skills/ knowledge do you need to acquire: (areas I need to develop) to prepare for this move?

Section D: Outline what legacy you want to leave from your career.

5.2 Find a mentor

A mentor is someone you respect and whose experiences you believe you can learn from. Before choosing a mentor here are some questions you need to ask yourself:

Questions to ask yourself when choosing a mentor

1. What do you want to learn or achieve?

2. How successful has this person been?

3. What makes you want to be mentored by this person?

4. Has this person ever mentored anyone before?

5. What communication skills does this person possess?

6. Will this person hold you accountable?

7. Will this person support you to be the best you can be?

8. Does this person have the time, energy and desire to mentor you?

9. Once you are satisfied with answers to these questions, you can then choose a suitable mentor for yourself.

Here are some questions you can use to facilitate a discussion with your mentor

Ask your mentor to tell a story from his or her career. Some questions to consider:

1. How did you land your current role?

2. Think back to five years ago. Did you envision this is where you would be?

3. Can you tell me about a time when you had a difficult boss? How did you handle it?

4. What's the most important leadership lesson you've learned and how is it valuable?

5. Tell me about a recent setback and how you recovered?

6. Was there ever a job position that you applied for and got, but you weren't 100% qualified?

Situations

Identify a challenging situation and share it with the mentor. Ask your mentor to act as a sounding board. Some questions to consider:

7. I'm considering a career transition. What do you see as the pros and cons?
8. Who are the people I need to align with in this organisation to achieve success?
9. How do you successfully stay connected to key influencers who do not work in same office or geographical area?
10. When trying to gain buy-in to implement a new programme, what tactics have worked for you?

Self-awareness

Ask a question that invites your mentor to contribute to your self-awareness. Some questions to consider:

11. Where do you see my strengths and what should I focus on to improve?
12. What do you see as some of my blind spots?
13. How do you think others perceive me?
14. How am I viewed by leadership?

Skill-building

Identify a skill you currently want to develop and ask your mentor for advice or resources. Some questions to consider:

15. How do you approach risk-taking?
16. What new skills do I need to move ahead?
17. How can I become a more assertive negotiator?
18. How can I become better at managing people who do not report to me?

"

You need to keep in mind that for a mentorship relationship to work you need to take ownership. That means:

- Scheduling meetings.
- Driving the agenda for the meetings.
- Being transparent on your needs and the assistance you require from your mentor.

"

Update your CV and
Linked in Profile

5.3 Make yourself visible in the job market through a professional CV and LinkedIn profile

Your CV and LinkedIn profile are the two key tools you use to introduce or present yourself to potential employers. Recruiters will often check your LinkedIn profile before inviting you for an interview. Here are some critical elements that will make your CV and LinkedIn profile appealing to recruiters, and land you an interview:

CV Checklist		LinkedIn Checklist	
Does your CV have precise and short personal details?		Choose a photo that shows your face clearly, that also conveys your personality.	
Does your CV have a clear vision or purpose statement?		Your headline must convey facts about you e.g. Legal *Secretary with Contracts Experience Seeking Next Challenge.*	
Does your CV have a list of skills (not too many, five max)?		Create a compelling LinkedIn Summary that tells the reader who you are and what you spend your time doing in just a few seconds.	
Do you have enough detail on your career history that shows the job you did, main responsibilities, systems/technology used, main achievements (not too long)?		List your main skills and get your friends to endorse that you possess that skill and verify it.	
Do you have the relevant key words relating to the job advertised to ensure you are shortlisted by the Applicant Tracking System?		Make your profile interesting by continuously engaging your followers through writing or sharing content about your industry.	

Preparing for
Interviews

5.4 How to prepare for interviews

When finding employment or changing jobs you cannot avoid the interview. So how do you ensure that you are ready for an interview when an opportunity presents itself ?

1. **Research the company conducting interviews**

    When preparing for an interview, the important information you need to know about the company is:

*   Their mission and vision

*   Their products

*   Their competitors

*   Their performance

*   Their social responsibility

You can obtain all this information on the company website. You can also read articles written about the company and its competitors.

2. **Research the job.** What you need to know about the job to do well in an interview is:

*   What are the expected outcomes of the job/What will you be expected to deliver?

*   What skills and experience do you need to have to do the job well?

*   Who are the key stakeholders that you will need to work with to deliver results? Your ability to deliver results will depend on how well you work with these people.

3. **Prepare your STAR questions.** Most companies use the competency-based interview model. Competency-based interviews (also called structured interviews) are interviews where each question is designed to test one or more specific skills. The answer is then matched against pre-decided criteria and marked accordingly. For example, the interviewers may want to test your ability to deal with stressful situations by asking first how the candidate generally handles stress and then asking the candidate to provide an example of a situation where he worked under pressure.

There is a specific way you need to answer these questions that is referred to as the STAR technique:

S = Situation	You need to provide an example of a situation in which you have had to demonstrate the skill. For example, a stressful situation you had to deal with.
T = Task	You need to explain what the task at hand was. What were you expected to deliver?
A = Action	You need to be able to discuss the actions you took to address the situation and do the task at hand. You need to explain what you did. In doing so, you will need to remember the following: • Be personal, i.e. talk about you, not the rest of the team. • Go into some detail. Do not assume that they will guess what you mean. • Steer clear of technical information, unless it is crucial to your story. • Explain what you did, how you did it, and why you did it.
R = Results	You need to discuss the outcomes of your actions. What did you achieve by adopting a particular action.

For each question you must be able to answer by demonstrating competence by structuring your answers in a STAR format. Here are some questions that you might come across – go ahead and use these questions to practise your answers using the STAR approach.

Question	S	T	A	R
Tell us about a time when you had to deal with a conflict within your team.				
Describe a situation where you had to deal with an angry customer.				
Tell us about the biggest change that you have had to deal with. How did you cope with it?				
What big decision did you make recently? How did you go about it?				
Describe a situation where you started off thinking that your approach was the best, but needed to alter your course during the implementation.				

When you get an opportunity to ask questions, you need to ask questions that will help you in deciding if the company/the job is a right choice for you. Below are some important questions you can ask that can help you determine that. You don't have to ask all of them. Pick one of two that are important to you at the time you are going for your interview.

Questions you can ask in an interview

Your Role: You want to find out as much about your role and responsibilities as you can. You obviously read the job description, but something like that doesn't always provide enough details of what your daily duties will be.

Use these questions to find out more about the position and your potential employer:

- **What do you look for in people who occupy this role?** You want to find out the most important traits the employer wants out of someone who takes this position. Do they value good time management? Punctuality? Perseverance? An outgoing personality? Asking this question is also a great opportunity for you to emphasise how your qualities make you a perfect candidate for this position. For example, if the interviewer talks about how they value someone who can solve problems, you can bring up times when you have helped tackle complicated issues in your previous jobs.

- **What does a typical day look like?** The online job description often doesn't provide the full details of your potential new position. Use this question to find out in what areas you will be needed the most and if you will stick to a schedule or be left to do the planning and scheduling yourself. An answer to this question will give you insight into the details of the job and will help you hit the ground running during your first few days once you've been offered the position. This is your chance to make sure the job is the right fit for you. However, use your judgment when asking this question. If you are interviewing with the Human Resources Manager of a large company, they may be unfamiliar with all of the daily duties of the position. If you are interviewing with your prospective team leader, they should be able to provide a detailed response.

- **Is this a new position or are you hiring to replace someone?** The answer to this question can be very insightful. A new position often means a company is growing. It can also indicate a role that might not yet be well-defined because no one has yet filled the role, and it will be up to you to shape what the role looks like if you are hired. If you are interviewing for an existing position, consider asking a follow-up question on why your predecessor left. This will help you discover if the company struggles with retaining employees and the kind of challenges that cause that.

- **What are the biggest challenges that come with this role?** We don't all enjoy dealing with similar challenges. Some people thrive when dealing with difficult customers while others might not be inspired by that. Asking this question gives you the opportunity to talk about the challenges that you have overcome in your past. Getting a realistic picture of the challenges you may face will help you manage your expectations should you be offered the job.

- **What are the most important milestones that you would like to see someone accomplish in the first few months?** This will give you an idea of what your employer would like to see out of you. It will also offer a glimpse of the things to come down the line and provide some insight on how you can potentially contribute to the company's growth.

- **Can you tell me about the company culture?** This question is important for you because you want to determine if you will fit into the culture. You will also be able to determine if you will enjoy working with the teams within the company.

Your future growth

With this question your intention is to check if the company believes and invests in employee growth. You also want to explore if the position you are interviewing for will provide you with growth opportunities in the future. Can you build a career from the job on offer?

- **Is there room for growth?** You want to make sure that you will not be stuck in a dead-end job. Look for something that will allow you to develop new skills while moving into different roles across the organisation. Find out how much time and effort you must put into your role before you can see real growth and change occur.

- **How are performance reviews done? How often do they occur?** Nothing helps someone grow like feedback from a performance review. At times you might not realise that you are underperforming or doing something wrong until someone points it out to you. Performance reviews give you a chance to know what you are doing well and what you need to improve on. Plus, a good performance review can usually come with the chance of a nice pay rise.

- **Does this position offer continued training or education?** Ongoing training and education is something that will help you learn new skills and ultimately become a better and more effective worker. Learning new skills will help you advance in the company and provide you with something that will be attractive to other employers if you ever decide to change jobs.

- **What is the next career that a person in this job can aspire to?** If other people in this position have moved onto bigger and better roles at the company, then it is a sure sign that there will be room for growth in your position.

The team

A team makes the culture of the department. Your intention with this question is to know what your potential co-workers are like and what it would be like to work with them.

- **Can you talk a little bit about the people I will be working with?** If the role calls for a lot of teamwork, you will want to know as much as you can about the people you might be working with. Even if the role is independent, you should still strive to find out more about the other employees.

- **Who will be the person I report to?** Your Team Leader is just as important as your co-workers in determining the culture of the team. In most instances, you will be talking to your Team Leader during the interview. This gives you an opportunity to find out about his/her leadership style and how he/she prefers to work with the team.

- **What other departments will I work with?** With the increase in collaboration at work you are most likely to be working with cross-functional teams. Your role might require you to interact and collaborate with other functions such as Marketing, Human Resources, Sales, or other departments.

The Interviewer

Making a good impression on your interviewer is of utmost importance. Ask them questions about their time and position at the company so that you can not only build rapport but get an idea of what working there is actually like.

- **How long have you been working here?** This is a pretty standard question but hearing about their backstory is always interesting. If they have been there for a long time, then you can find out more about the company culture from them.

- **What do you like most about working here?** The interviewer will share with you the positive selling points about the company that she/he likes. It could be good pay, benefits, or a fun company culture. Look for signs that the company will support your career growth, promote a healthy work/life balance, and appreciate your hard work.

Pay and benefits

This is one area of the interviews that always has controversial views. Do you ask about the salary or don't you? My take is that by the time you attend the interview you should at least have an idea of how much the job pays. It would have been indicated to you by the recruiter. If they are not forthcoming with pay information ask them before you attend an interview. This way, you avoid wasting your time. Imagine if the job is paying less than you currently earn and you only find out when the company makes an offer to you.

Be clear about the benefits you currently have and types of benefits that are important to you. The main benefits normally offered by most employers are:

- **Holidays and time off:** In most countries employers are required by law to offer annual holiday pay. There are also statutory entitlements to other types of time off, including maternity, paternity, adoption and parental leave.

- **Pension:** Most companies offer you a pension scheme which is just a type of savings plan to help you save money for later life.

- **Health care and risk benefits:** Benefits relating to health care insurance. These vary greatly depending on your country and your employer.

- **Company car and car allowances:** These also vary depending on your job and your employer offering.

- **Other benefits:** Some employers may offer a diverse range of other employee benefits including childcare benefits (such as on-site nurseries), concierge services, free or subsidised staff canteens and gym membership.

You could ask the following questions about pay and benefits:

- **What is your pay philosophy?** Most companies have this – it's the pay principles approved by Directors that guide on how the company wants to compensate its employees. It covers things like how the company wants to compete in the market – where they want to position themselves on the pay scale in the market. It also covers things like annual pay increases. Will you get a performance-based pay rise or is it negotiated and agreed?

- **What benefit offering does the company pride itself on?** This allows the company to flesh out benefits they believe attract the best talent in the market.

- **How does your performance influence your pay?** This gives you an indication of whether the company values performance and if you can influence your pay through your work.

- **How flexible are their pay practices?** With this question you want to find out if everyone gets similar benefits or if you have a choice to personalise benefits according to what's important to you and your lifestyle.

The Final Steps

Now that the interview is coming to a close, you should make sure you end with some strong questions that will leave a good impression.

- **Based on what you have seen, do you have any doubts about my ability to fulfil this role?** This will not only show confidence but will also help the interviewer soothe any lingering doubts that they might have about your performance. At worst, they could provide you with some constructive feedback about your abilities.

- **When can I expect to hear back from you?** Most employers will typically get back to you within a week. If you haven't heard back from them, then it's likely they aren't considering you for the job. It is a good idea to check if it is okay for you to follow-up with the interviewer in case you do not hear from them within a specified time.

- **When does the job start?** This provides an opportunity to discuss notice periods and realistic start dates from both your perspective and the employer's perspective. It will help you with your planning, if you know the start dates or potential roles that you have interviewed for you can make plans to take time off before you begin with a new employer.

- **What is the next step in the hiring process?** This should be your last question. Hopefully the answer will give you clues as to whether the company is considering other candidates. Also, by asking this question, you've shown the employer that you are interested in pursuing the position and are willing to take the next step. Would you be hired right away or are there more steps? Perhaps you need to take part in a follow-up interview or need to participate in a background check.

5.5 Prepare for your first 90 days of success

Once you have been hired in a job that you have worked hard to secure, you want to make sure that you have a strong start. Below are activities to focus on to ensure you have a strong start:

Before you start

* Review all of the research you did on the organisation when you were preparing for interviews. Re-read the organisation's website, and notes you took during your interview.

Day 1

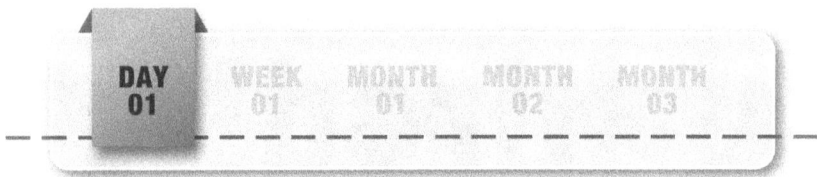

* Today is all about absorbing as much information as you can. Make it your goal to listen 90% of the time and talk 10% of the time. Most of the talking should be asking questions.

* Make sure you take notes. There will be a lot of information shared with you which is nearly impossible to remember. Important things to take note of include co-workers' names, job titles, and something memorable about your interaction with them; information about the organisation that you won't be able to find in documentation later on; and little nuggets of wisdom you might receive from new colleagues. Do not worry about capturing everything. Much of what you hear on the first day will make more sense as you begin your job responsibilities.

* Set up your work space. Depending on your job, this might mean getting your computer set up, getting usernames and passwords to access all the internal systems and getting all the necessary office supplies and furniture, or getting the right uniform or tools.

The first week

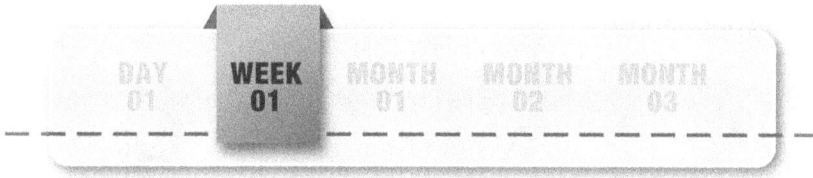

- Ask your manager to set up getting-to-know-you meetings with key stakeholders, that are your internal customers (colleagues), and ask your key stakeholders about their expectations from your role. You can learn a lot about stakeholders' expectations of you this way!

- Practise humility. In your first week, learn about how things are done. Recognise what is working well and take note of areas that can be improved. Try not to fix anything at this stage unless specifically asked to. While your intention is to come with a fresh perspective, your focus during this period is to learn about the organisation and acknowledge what's working while taking note of what needs to be improved. A good rule of thumb is to avoid talking about your most recent job as much as possible

The first month

- Continue with key stakeholders' meetings and getting to know your new employer better through reading your newsletters, websites, social media, and annual reports – anything you can find.

- Have a frank discussion with your manager about any unwritten rules or standards. You can also seek clarification on performance metrics and expectations.

- Update your social networking profiles. Let everyone know about your new job, and any new ways you might want to connect with them.

The second month

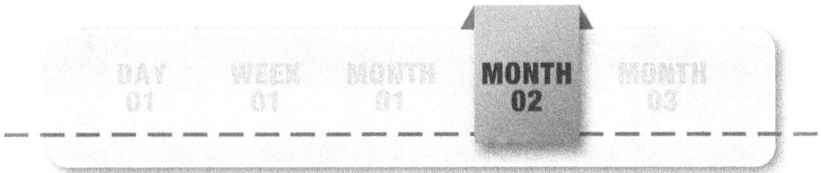

- Accelerate your learning about the organisation, their products, services, technologies, as well as markets. Create a systematic way that will help you to learn as much as you can about the organisation.

- Focus on improving your networks. Subscribe to relevant blogs, join professional associations or Meetup groups.

- Seek out a mentor or sponsor within the organisation. Having a mentor (or several) can improve your job performance, grow your network, and even help you advance more quickly within your organisation.

The third month

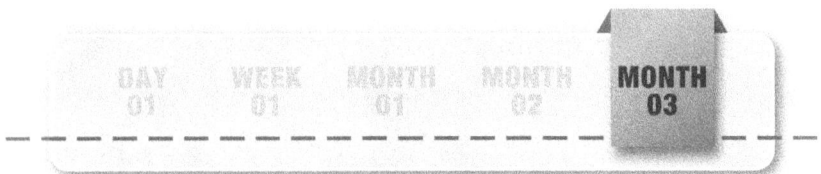

- Accelerate your value contribution: during the first two months you identified areas that required improvement and you have been discussing these with your team leader. Now it's time to act on all your suggestions. You might have noticed a task you have to do over and over again? Perhaps you can automate it. Is there a particular workflow you've found difficult to master? Maybe it could be made more intuitive. Whatever you decide to do, make sure you align with everyone who is involved or impacted by the change or improvement you are suggesting. Gain their buy-in and make sure it doesn't impede their work!

- Focus on your personal brand and build credibility: be clear on what brand you want to create. What do you want to be known for? Do you want to be known as the person who is reliable, who delivers against commitment, who is knowledgeable in your area of expertise? Whatever your personal brand ambition is, be clear about it and act towards creating the impression you want people to have about you.

- Seek feedback from your team leader and some of the key stakeholders you have been working with. Such feedback can be in a form of direct discussion. Try and simplify the process of asking for feedback. People avoid giving feedback in a formal way. A simple discussion focusing on the following will suffice:

  - what they see working well in your area.

  - where they think you or your team is getting stuck in meeting their needs.

  - what they think you can do differently to meet their needs.

Prepare for this discussion, take notes, be grateful for the feedback. It is important that you act on the feedback you received.

Works Cited

1   Buckingham, M. *Go put your strengths to work: six powerful steps to achieve outstanding performance.* London: Simon & Schuster, 2007.

2   Gallup. How Millenials want to live and work. gallup.com [online], [cited 2018 September 2016. Available from: https://www.gallup.com/workplace/238073/millennials-work-live.aspx

3   Szuczuka, T. *Pursuit of passionate purpose: success strategies for a rewarding personal and business life.* New Jersey: John Wiley, 2015.

4   Buckingham, M. *Standout. 2.0: Assess your strengths. Find your edge. Win at work.* Boston: Harvard Business Review Press, 2015.

5   Green, R. *Mastery.* Glasgow: Bell & Bain Ltd, 2012.

6   Garcia, H and Miralles, F. *Ikigai: The Japanese secret to a long and happy life.* London: Hutchinson, 2017.

7   Sone, O., Nakaya, N., Ohmori, K., Shimazu, T., Higashiguchi, M., Kakizaki, M., Kikuchi, N., Kuriyama, S., Kakizaki, M., Tsuji, I. Sense of life worth living (Ikigai) and mortality in Japan: Ohsaki Study. *Psychosomatic Medicine*, 70 (6): 709-715, 2008.

8   Csikzentmihalya, M. *Flow and the foundations of positive psychology: The collected works of Mihaly Csikzentmihalya.* London: 2014.

9   Holland, J.L. *Making vocational choices: a theory of careers.* NJ: Prentice Hall, 1997.

10 Bolles R. *What color is your parachute?: A practical manual for job hunters and career-changers.* CA: Ten Speed, 2016.

11 O'Keefe, P.A., Dweck C.S. and Walton, G.M. Implicit theories of interest: finding your passion or developing it. [Online]; [cited 2018 September 7]; 29 (10): Available from: https://doi. org/10.1177%2F0956797618780643.

12 Gladwell, M. *Outliers: The Story of Success.* London: Penguin Books, 2009.

13 Sandberg, S. *Lean In: Women, Work and the Will to Lead.* London: W.H. Allen, 2015.

14 Quinn, R. and Cameron, S. *Culture Typology.* [Online].; 2018 [cited 2018 September 13]. Available from: https://www.quinnassociation.com/en/ culture typology.

15 Deloitte. Human Capital Trends: the rise of social enterprise. Deloitte. com. [Online]: Deloitte, 2018 [cited 2018 September 13. Available from: https://w w w2.deloitte.com/content/dam/insights/us/articles/ HCTrends2018/2018-HCtrends_Rise-of-the-social- enterprise.pdf.

16 Hagel, J., Schwartz, J., and Bersin, J. Navigating the future of work: Can we point business, workers and social institutions in the same direction? *Deloitte Review*. [online]; 2017 [cited 2018 September 13. Available from: https:// documents. deloitte.com/insights/ DeloitteReview21.

17 Ibarra, H. Working Identity: Unconventional strategies for reinventing your career. Boston: *Harvard Business Press*, 2003.

18 Llopis, G. 5 ways a legacy-driven mindset will define your leadership. Forbes. com. [Online], 2014 [cited 2018 13 September. Available from: https://www. forbes.com/sites/glennllopis/2014/02/20/5-ways-a-legacy-driven-mindset-will-define-your-leadership/#1334096616b1.

19 Burchard, B. *The Millionaire Messenger*. London: Simon & Schuster, 2011.

20 Reed, B. and Attwell, M. The rise of the expert economy: could sharing wisdom be the next gig? [Online].; 2018 [cited 2018 August 10. Available from: http:// civicenterprises.net/MediaLibrary/Docs/ ExpertEconomy.pdf.

21 PwC. *The Sharing Economy*. pwc.co.uk. [Online].; 2014 [cited 2018 August 13. Available from: https:// www.pwc.fr/fr/assets/files/pdf/2015/05/pwc_etude_ sharing_economy.pdf.

22 McKinsey. Independent work: choices, necessity and the gig economy. McKinsey. com. [Online].; 2016 [cited 2018 September 12. Available from: https://www. mckinsey.com/~/media/McKinsey/Featured%20Insights/Employment%20 and%20Growth/ Independent%20work%20Choice%20necessity%20 and%20 the%20gig%20economy/Independent-Work-Choice-necessity-and-the-gig-economy-Executive- Summary.ashx.

23 Mulcahy, D. *The gig economy: The complete guide to getting better work, taking more time off and financing the life you want*. Special Ed. London: Amacom, 2016.

24 World Economic Forum. The Future of jobs: employment, skills and workforce strategy for the fourth industrial revolution. [Online].; 2016 [cited 2018 September 13. Available from: http://www3.weforum. org/docs/ WEF_FOJ Executive_Summary_Jobs.pdf.

25 European commission, ICT for work: Digital skills in the workplace.ec.europa. eu. [Online].; 2017. Available from: https://ec.europa.eu/digital-single-market/ en/ news/ict-work-digital-skills-workplace.

26 CultureWizard. Trends in global virtual teams. Culturewizard.com. [Online], 2016 [cited 2018 September 13. Available from: http://cdn.culturewizard.com/ PDF/Trends_in_VT_Report_4-17-2016.pdf.

27 Global Workplace Analytics. Telecommuting data. globalworkplaceanalytics. com. [Online].; 2018 [cited 2018 September 13. Available from: https:// globalworkplaceanalytics.com/ telecommuting-statistics.

28 McKinsey Global Institute. The digital future of work: What skills will be needed? mckinsey.com. [Online].; 2017 [cited 2018 September 13. Available from: https:// www.mckinsey.com/featured-insights/future-of-work/ the-digital-future-of-work-what-skills-will-be-needed

29   McKinsey. Jobs lost jobs gained : Workforce transitions in a time of automation. McKinsey.com [online] [cited 2018 September 13. Available from: https://www. mckinsey.com/~/media/mckinsey/featured%20insights/Future%20of%20 Organizations/What%20the%20future%20of%20work%20will%20mean%20 for%20jobs%20skills%20and%20wages/MGI-Jobs-Lost-Jobs-Gained-Report-December-6-2017.ashx

30   Gray D. Robot revolution: AI and the future of work: Will the rise of artificial intelligence make you more or less likely to find your dream job? economist. com. [Online].; 2016 [cited 2018 09 20. Available from: http://shapingthefuture. economist.com/robot-revolution-ai-and-the-future-of-work/.

31   Bessen J. *Automation and Jobs: When Technology Boosts Employment.* Boston University School of Law – Law & Economics. 2017 April 12.

32   Tapscott D., Tapscott A. *Blockchain Revolution: How the technology behind Bitcoin and other cryptocurrencies is changing the world.* London: Portfolio Penguin; 2016.

33   Open Access News. The rise and future of Blockchain [Online].; 2017 [cited 2018 09 20. Available from: https://www.openaccessgovernment.org/ the-rise-and-future-of-blockchain/38956/.

34   Global jobcoin. globaljobcoin.com. [Online].; 2017 [cited 2018 September 13. Available from: https://www.globaljobcoin.com/media/files/documents/ GJC Whitepaper.pdf.

35   Bersin J. Catch the wave: the 21st century career. [Online].; 2017 [cited 2018 September 13. Available from: https://www2.deloitte.com/insights/us/en/ deloitte-review/issue-21/changing-nature-of-careers- in-21st-century.html.

Index

www.ingramcontent.com/pod-product-compliance
Lightning Source LLC
Chambersburg PA
CBHW050106210326
41519CB00015BA/3849